MW00581100

Genesis 1 and the Creationism Debate

Genesis 1 and the Creationism Debate

Being Honest to the Text,
Its Author, and His Beliefs

Steven DiMattei

WIPF & STOCK · Eugene, Oregon

GENESIS 1 AND THE CREATIONISM DEBATE
Being Honest to the Text, Its Author, and His Beliefs

Wipf & Stock
An Imprint of Wipf and Stock Publishers
199 W. 8th Ave., Suite 3
Eugene, OR 97401

www.wipfandstock.com

PAPERBACK ISBN 13: 978-1-4982-3132-9
HARDCOVER ISBN 13: 978-1-4982-3134-3

Manufactured in the U.S.A.   03/29/2016

Bible translations are the author's. Hebrew transliterations are simplified and presented without vowel markings for ease of reading.

Satellite photo of Earth courtesy of NASA

Illustration of Genesis 1:6–14 by Bob Kayganich.

Contents

Introduction

Creationism is not something new. The belief that the world was created by an omnipotent being or beings has been around for millennia and has taken on numerous different forms and expressions.[1] One might even argue that such beliefs are hardwired into the human psyche. That as sentient beings whose natural tendency is to organize and rationalize the world that we perceive, we, or better yet our ancestors quite naturally composed stories about the nature and origin of the world that they perceived and experienced.

While this book does not necessarily contest such beliefs, it does challenge modern proponents of this belief who, for a variety of reasons, think that their beliefs about the nature of the world and its origin are founded and legitimated by a text, a creation story, that was written more than two thousand five hundred years ago. This is quite bewildering in and of itself when we stop to think about it. How can anyone living in the twenty-first century with our twenty-first-century perception, knowledge, and experience of the world honestly claim that they adhere to beliefs forged by a people and culture that lived more than two thousand five hundred years ago? Are these people being honest to themselves? And more importantly for our present purpose, are they being honest to these ancient texts and the claims and beliefs of their authors?

The biblical texts themselves will make a formal response to these questions in the forthcoming chapters, where it will be demonstrated that modern day Creationists do not actually believe in the beliefs and claims represented in these ancient texts. A large part of the problem is that like many modern "readers" of the Bible's texts, Creationists actually know little

---

1. There are a number of good anthologies that can be consulted: Sproul, *Primal Myths*; Hamilton, *In the Beginning*; and Leeming, *Dictionary of Creation Myths*.

to nothing about these texts, the beliefs and messages of their individual authors, and the historical and literary contexts that shaped those beliefs.

Ancient stories that explained the nature and origin of the world and its phenomena, as chapter 1's close reading of Genesis 1 and 2 will reveal, were shaped by how ancient cultures and peoples perceived and experienced their world. This is readily apparent to anyone who has read the Bible's creation narratives on the terms of their authors and the cultural contexts that produced them. The author of Genesis 1, for example, composed a creation narrative that explained how the world as *he and his culture perceived it* came into existence. And this author and his larger ancient Near Eastern culture perceived their world as surrounded by water—water above the sky, which gave it its blue color, and water below the earth upon which it rested. They perceived and accepted as "truth" that the sky held back the waters above it, that the moon produced its own light, that the day itself was the source of daylight and not the sun, that human beings were essentially of the divine as opposed to the animals of the earth, and that the seventh day was inherently created holy and consecrated by the creator deity at creation. These beliefs about the nature of *their* world, these culturally conditioned "truths" as it were, shaped the composition of this author's creation story so that the god of Genesis 1 is portrayed *creating the very world that its author and culture perceived*—a moon that produced light, the creation of light separate from the sun, an explanation of how earth emerged from the waters below and became surrounded by the waters above, and how these waters were kept in place by the sky which the creator deity specifically made for this purpose, an explanation of why the seventh day after each new moon and each consecutive seventh day thereafter were inherently sacred, and so forth.

In other words, this author's creation narrative was shaped by *his* experience and perception of the world. This is what the text itself reveals when read on its own terms and from within its own historical and literary contexts—not on the terms, contexts, nor beliefs of later readers. Obviously this also means acknowledging that we in the twenty-first century neither perceive nor experience the world in the terms depicted in this ancient text by its author. So how is it then that a group of individuals in today's day and age can claim that their beliefs about the world and its origin are substantiated by the perceptions, experiences, and limited knowledge of the world as held by an author and culture that existed two thousand five hundred years ago? In short they cannot and do not.

The fact of the matter is that Creationists pontificate on their own beliefs and agenda with little to no knowledge of the actual texts of Genesis 1 and 2, the beliefs of their authors and *their* messages, the cultural circumstances that shaped those beliefs and messages, and the literary conventions employed by these authors in composing their creation stories. In this regard the real debate is not between science and religion. This book is not a scientific counterargument against Creationism. Rather the real point of contention is between modern or traditional beliefs and perceptions *about* these ancient texts, and what the texts themselves reveal about their own compositional nature and the beliefs and perceptions of their authors. Thus, one of the central aims of this book is to present readers with an accurate, unbiased, and culturally contextualized presentation of the beliefs and worldview of the author of Genesis 1, and to explain why this author believed what he did by referencing his cultural context. After all, this is a book about *his* beliefs as expressed through his composition—not those of later readers.

We additionally need to start acknowledging that religious views and beliefs change. This can easily be verified by studying the religious texts of the past in chronological fashion. And since the collection of texts that only centuries later became the Bible span a thousand years, we can see these changes in the biblical canon itself. Changes in religious ideas and beliefs are usually prompted by changing social, political, phenomenological, and even psychological factors. Since religion often deals with explaining the observable world *as a particular culture perceived it* by referencing unseen forces, gods, or God, we easily understand how, for example, it was once commonplace to explain the origins of thunder, fertility, agriculture, illnesses, natural disasters, etc. as originating from the gods or a God—beliefs still visible in the oldest layers of the Bible! However as cultures progressed and knowledge about the natural world increased, these phenomena were no longer explained by having recourse to unseen forces, beings, or God. The Bible as an anthology of ancient literature written by roughly sixty-some different authors and scribal guilds spanning a time period of a thousand years and across two radically different cultures bears witness to these very changes, and even competing belief systems and worldviews.[2] We need to start being honest to these once independent texts and their authors by reading and understanding them each on their own terms and from within

2. The topic of my forthcoming book, *Understanding Bible Contradictions: Why They're There and What They Tell Us about the Bible and the Men Who Wrote It.*

their own unique historical and literary contexts, and not through the theological constructs and beliefs of later readers.

BEING HONEST TO THE TEXTS AND THEIR AUTHORS

The subtitle of this book identifies our main objective as readers of the biblical text. Indeed, being honest to the Bible's texts, their authors, and their beliefs should be our first, and in many regards our only, priority and goal. Believe it or not, however, this is often not the case at all. Often the Bible's texts are read in such a way as to support a completely different agenda—legitimating *the reader's beliefs about* the text.

Thus, it might initially be asked: what exactly does being honest to the texts and their authors mean, and conversely not mean? Furthermore, why is it that Creationists are neither honest to the texts nor their authors, although they would have you believe otherwise?

In general it might be said that being honest to the biblical texts and their authors means just that. It means that the biblical texts and the beliefs, worldviews, ideologies, culturally formed perceptions, and even biases of their individual authors are our object of study. It means that our task, even obligation I would argue, is to read and understand these texts on the terms of the texts themselves, not on the terms, beliefs, nor contexts of later readers. It means understanding these ancient documents as their authors intended and as products of their own unique historical, cultural, and literary worlds. It means understanding what the texts say and perhaps more importantly do not say, and even why they say what they do. It means objectively identifying and understanding the beliefs and views of the authors of these texts, their original purposes for writing their texts, and in response to what historical circumstances, to whom, and in the context of what other literary works. In other words, the focus of our investigation are the texts, what the texts themselves reveal about their compositional nature, their authors, their historical and literary contexts, and their cultural worldviews and beliefs—and not what later readers have been conditioned to claim, believe, or think *about* these texts as the result of later interpretive frameworks and theological constructs.

In many regards, then, being honest to the texts requires that we distinguish between what the texts say on their own terms and as products of their own unique historical worlds, and what later readers have claimed or continue to claim *about* these texts. Being honest to the texts themselves, in other words, does not mean starting from theological or interpretive assumptions handed down to us by later interpretive traditions, such as those embedded in this collection of ancient literature's title, "the Holy Bible." This and similar interpretive frameworks are reader-oriented, theological constructs that were created centuries after these texts were written and to suit the needs and purposes of later readers. That is to say, the label "the Holy Bible" and the ideas and beliefs implied in this label—namely, that the text is the word of God, that it is a homogenous inerrant narrative or revelation, a unified doctrine of salvation history, etc.—represent the beliefs and theological convictions of *later readers* and how *they*, guided by their own theological concerns, perceived these texts, now conceptualized as a text in the singular, indeed as a holy book. Being honest to the texts and their authors, then, requires us to move backwards in time to the texts and their original contexts *before* they were co-opted for different purposes and meanings by later readers who imposed their own beliefs, labels, prejudices, and theological constructs onto this collection of ancient literature. Being honest to the texts puts the texts in their original contexts as our first priority.

Thus, like any field of study, knowing the meaning of these ancient texts, what their authors believed and why, what historical crisis or concerns were they writing in response to, etc., requires education. It requires possessing knowledge about ancient literature in general, about the historical contexts of texts written from approximately the eighth century BCE to the first century CE and from within two vastly different cultural contexts, the ancient Near East and the Greco-Roman world. It requires knowing the literature of these two cultures, and the literary genres they shared with our biblical scribes. It requires knowledge about who wrote ancient texts in general, why, and to whom. It requires knowledge about the literary precursors that our biblical scribes used in composing their texts, and so on. When modern readers profess to know the meaning of these ancient texts while ignoring or lacking this knowledge, what they are in fact doing is merely professing *their own subjective beliefs about the text*. They are spouting *their* meaning of the text and not the meaning of these texts per their authors. More than often they are professing a meaning of the text that accords with what the label "the Holy Bible" has come to mean to these readers personally, and not the meaning of these texts according to their once independent authors.

Of course, a Fundamentalist might respond by saying that the proper meaning and understanding of the Bible's texts only come through divine guidance or inspiration, usually understood at the whims of the reader. But this is precisely my point: this and similar such interpretive frameworks are all reader-oriented, subjective constructs imposed upon these ancient texts centuries after they were written, and by a readership that possessed little to no knowledge about ancient literature in general and the historical contexts that produced these texts in particular. In this and similar scenarios, the starting point for the so-called "reading" of these ancient texts becomes the reader's own subjective or inherited beliefs *about the text*, and not the texts themselves! Although this is an important part in understanding how later readers came to view this collection of ancient literature as the word of God,[3] in this book we are interested in *what the texts themselves reveal* about their own compositional nature and the beliefs of their authors long before they were co-opted by later readers and impregnated with new meanings, beliefs, and theological frameworks. Reproducing, understanding, and even defending the beliefs and messages of the authors of these ancient texts—against those of later readers—is one of this book's central aims.

Thus I often find myself articulating that my aim is *to defend* the biblical texts, their authors, and their beliefs. This means that I am not interested in defending the beliefs, views, and agendas of later readers or faith communities, or the theological assumptions and beliefs implied in the label "the Holy Bible." These are all the apologist's agenda. As a biblical scholar my interests and aims are the beliefs of the authors who penned these ancient texts, to understand them, and to faithfully and objectively reproduce them. After all, this is not a book about my beliefs *about* these texts. Neither is it a book about the reader's beliefs *about* these texts. Rather, it is a book about the beliefs and messages of the authors who penned these ancient texts long before they were edited together by later scribes and impregnated with new meanings by later readers who simply created new interpretive frameworks through which to "read" these ancient texts. Thus defending these once independent texts, their individual authors, and their unique beliefs is quite different from defending what is implied and often understood in the label "the Holy Bible." These are two completely separate and even opposing aims. The latter advocates an understanding and "reading"

---

3. See my forthcoming, *The Making of God's Book: How a Collection of Competing and Contradictory Texts Became the Word of God.*

of these texts through the theological lens of later readers where that which is implied in the label "the Holy Book" becomes the dominant message of these texts, now conceived as a text in the singular, while the former advocates being honest to the biblical texts on the terms of their individual authors and the cultural contexts that produced them *before* these texts were appropriated by later readers to be "read" through later interpretive and theological frameworks.

What I am proposing then is that the biblical texts themselves, each independently, become our object of study and each from within their own cultural context, so that it is *the texts themselves* in comparative study that reveal what they are and conversely are not, that reveal what their authors believed and conversely did not, that reveal the literary techniques employed by these ancient scribes in legitimating their beliefs, and so forth. In this paradigm learning about what these individual authors believed themselves, why they believed what they did, and the historical and literary circumstances that shaped those beliefs become our primary goal—not the varied and subjective beliefs of readers living centuries later. More specifically, this book is about the beliefs and worldview of the author of Genesis 1, regardless of the beliefs or non-beliefs of its modern readers. The point is not our beliefs *about* the text, but the author's. Allowing this ancient document to invite us into *its* worldview—rather than imposing ours onto it—is our main objective. And this is accomplished by reading the text on its own terms and as a product of its own historical and literary context—not on the terms nor contexts of later readers and later interpretive frameworks.

1

Genesis' Two Creation Accounts

My goals in this chapter are threefold: (1) to put forward the textual data that convincingly demonstrate the hand of two different authors for Genesis 1:1—2:3 and 2:4b—3:24; (2) to demonstrate that the depiction of the creation of the world and of mankind in both these accounts were conditioned and shaped by subjective and culturally formed beliefs and ideas about the nature of the world as perceived by the ancient scribes who wrote these accounts. They are not, in other words, divinely dictated, divinely inspired, nor intended as objective/scientific descriptions of the world and its origin. This is not a subjective claim that I am making; rather, it is an objective claim that will be supported by the forthcoming textual data and what the texts themselves reveal about their authors' beliefs and worldviews. Lastly (3), to expose why the claims made by modern day Creationists about Genesis 1 and 2 are disingenuous and negligent of the very beliefs and claims made in these ancient texts by their authors. As we shall see, this is primarily because Creationists are actually ignorant about what these texts themselves advocate, of why they advocate what they do, of their authors' individual beliefs and worldviews, of the historical and literary contexts within which these texts were produced, and of the larger ancient Near Eastern cultural perspectives and beliefs about the nature of the world that influenced and shaped the compositions of Genesis 1 and 2.

Creationists, and Fundamentalists in general, need to stop treating these ancient documents as empty shells in which modern beliefs and viewpoints are capriciously inserted with no regard for nor knowledge about the very beliefs of the ancient scribes who penned these texts, their culturally shaped perspectives, and the historical and literary circumstances that produced these texts in the first place. Our goal throughout this chapter is to let these ancient texts invite us into their worldview, and to understand that world as objectively as possible—not to manipulate these ancient documents so that they conform to our beliefs, our perceptions, and our scientific knowledge about the world.

GENESIS 1:1—2:3 AND 2:4B—3:24: AN OVERVIEW

Ancient and modern readers alike have long recognized the differences between the seven-day creation account of Genesis 1:1—2:3 and the garden of Eden account of Genesis 2:4b—3:24. Even on stylistic grounds noticeable in an English translation, the first creation account is lofty, formulaic, structured, heaven-centered, and awe-inspiring with its image of a transcendent and impersonal creator deity who brings creation and order into existence by the mere force of his word. The second creation account, on the other hand, is informal and fable-like in its presentation, anthropologically oriented, earth-centered, dramatic, and theologically more poignant with its etiological tale describing how man, crafted from the clay of the earth and prompted by a talking serpent, fell from the presence of his creator, and as a result human suffering and toil befell the lot of mankind.

But the most noticeable differences, indeed contradictions, lie in their presentation of the order of creation *and* the manner through which man and woman come into existence. For instance, the first account describes how God creates—the Hebrew verb used is *bara'*—plants on the third day (1:11), then animals on the fifth and sixth days (1:20–25), and lastly male and female together in the image and likeness of the creator god (1:26–27), thus displaying how mankind is vastly different from the animals (more below). The repeated emphasis is on a god who creates (*bara'*) by pronouncing the thing into existence, separating it out, and then claiming the goodness in the created thing and by extension in the created order of the world. Spatial and temporal order, as well as a formulaic style, are hallmarks of this first creation account.

We find none of these features in the second creation account. Rather, we are now informed that Yahweh (here the deity's name is specified) *first* forms or molds—the Hebrew verb is *yatsar*—man from the dust of the earth (2:7), then plants (2:9), and then so that the man should not be alone,

Yahweh molds (*yatsar*) animals from the earth that are in essence similar to the man (2:18–19), but since man is unable to find a satisfactory companion among the animals, woman is built (*banah*) from the man's rib (2:22). Thus in our first account plants and animals are created (*bara'*) *before* both male and female are created together in the image of the god(s), while in the latter account man is molded (*yatsar*) from the ground first, *then* plants and animals, *and then*, woman is built from the man's rib as a response to the man's inability to find a suitable counterpart among the animals that were also fashioned (*yatsar*) from the ground.

Wordplay and puns are also unique to this second creation account, and help accentuate this account's anthropological orientation and the views of its author. For instance, we are told that from the ground (*'adamah*) Yahweh molds the man (*'adam*), but no other beast formed from the ground (*'adamah*) has a name, that is, a corresponding essence, similar to the man's; only woman does: "This now is bone from my bones and flesh from my flesh. Accordingly she shall be called 'woman' (*'ishah*) because from man (*'ish*) she was taken" (2:23). In the first account, male and female are created together in the image of the deity and his divine council ("let us make," "in our image" [1:26]). But in the second account, the creation of man and woman is presented separately; and through the use of wordplay their essences, that is, the created stuff from which each one was fashioned, is highlighted: man (*'adam*) comes from the ground (*'adamah*), woman (*'ishah*) from man (*'ish*). We will see below that these two distinct perspectives and messages reveal how each one of our authors variously viewed, and thus uniquely composed a narrative about, the nature of man and woman.

One of the most prominent and distinguishable differences between these two creation accounts, especially in the Hebrew, is the manner in which each creation account depicts the creator god. Genesis 1:1—2:3 refers to the deity with the Hebrew word for god (*'elohim*) in all thirty-five of its occurrences. The second account, Genesis 2:4b–24, refers to the deity as Yahweh in all eleven occurrences.[1] This is in line with the larger textual

1. The divine name for Israel's god, Yahweh (transliterated as *yhwh*), is rendered in the majority of English translations as LORD. This practice, which is misleading as well as misrepresentative of the Hebrew text, follows a late Judaic oral tradition of substituting the Hebrew *adonai* (lord) for *yhwh* in the reading of the Torah, since later Judaism—centuries after these texts were actually composed—conceived of the name as sacred and unspeakable. Modern translation practices have regrettably chosen to follow this later oral tradition rather than the actual Hebrew text! Here, we will be as honest to the

traditions from which these two creation accounts originated. In the textual tradition to which the first creation account belongs (ch. 2), the name Yahweh is not used nor is it known until it is revealed to Moses at Sinai.[2] Not so for the textual tradition to which this second account belongs; it always uses the personal name Yahweh and contradictorily professes that the name Yahweh was known and invoked throughout the whole patriarchal era.[3] This is just one example of contradictory authorial agendas and theologies between these two textual traditions.[4]

Along with the different terms for the creator god, both texts also portray their deity in strikingly different manners. In the first creation account God speaks things into existence. He is presented as majestic and utterly transcendent; he never interacts with his creation and stands completely outside of it. In the second creation account, by contrast, Yahweh is consistently portrayed in anthropomorphic terms and communicates and interacts directly with his creation (and often with himself in the form of interior monologues).[5] Such anthropomorphism, that is, presenting a deity in human terms, is visible throughout this creation account. Yahweh *molds* man from the dust of the earth, presumably with his hands (2:7),[6] *breathes* into the man's nostrils, *plants* a garden (2:8), *takes* and *puts* the man in the garden (2:15), *commands* the man (2:16), *molds* animals from the ground (2:19), *builds* a woman from the man's rib (2:22), *walks* in the garden (3:8), *calls* and *speaks* to his creation (3:9, 13–14), *makes* garments of skins for the human pair (3:21), and lastly *puts* the human pair outside the garden (3:23). This type of anthropomorphism is never found in the first creation account's portrait of God, and neither throughout the textual tradition of which this creation account stood as its opening statement (ch. 2). Rather it is a unique feature of the author of the second creation account.

Hebrew text as possible. Thus everywhere your English translation has LORD in small caps, the Hebrew manuscript has Yahweh, or more precisely יהוה.

2. See Gen 17:1; 28:3; 35:11; 48:3; and Exod 6:2–3—all from the Priestly textual tradition (ch. 2).

3. See Gen 4:26; 12:3–8; 13:4; 15:7, etc.—all from the Yahwist textual tradition.

4. The Bible's various and at times competing textual traditions and how they relate to one another is the topic of my forthcoming book, *Understanding Bible Contradictions: Why They're There and What They Tell Us about the Bible and the Men Who Wrote It*.

5. See Gen 2:18; 3:22; 6:3; 8:21–22; 18:17–19, etc.

6. Cf. The image of Yahweh as a potter fashioning man with his hands (Isa 64:8). See also Isa 29:16 where the verb *yatsar* is likewise used to describe the act of forming man from clay, like a potter does.

In addition to the varying portraits of the creator deity, there are other differences that set these two accounts apart. Where one attempts to give an orderly explanation of the creation of the then known world via the word of an all-powerful transcendent deity, and in short is heaven-centered, the other attempts to answer questions of an anthropological nature, is earth-centered, and solely focuses on man's creation, relationship, disobedience toward, and finally expulsion from a very personal and "human" deity, Yahweh. It might furthermore be said that the first creation myth, for reasons that will be explored below, moves from chaos to order, darkness to light, and formlessness to form, within which there are repeated refrains where God pronounces the inherent goodness in the created thing and finally blesses humanity—a humanity that is both male and female and created together in the image and likeness of their divine creator(s).

The second account, on the other hand, moves from an infertile, barren, and humanless landscape through the formation of man from this ground, his placement in a fertile and fecund garden, the formation of woman from the man's rib, to finally their expulsion from the garden and (re)placement on a ground that has now become cursed (Gen 3:17; 4:11; 5:29). Unlike the former's original state of creation which is represented as a surging watery abyss enveloped in darkness, the latter's original state of creation depicts a waterless earth with no rain nor vegetation (Gen 2:5); it represents the dry, arid land of the geography of Canaan. The toil required for man ('adam) to work this dry, hard soil ('adamah) is a prominent theme in this story. In other words, it is an etiological tale which attempts to provide a rationale for man's current lot, as perceived by its author and his culture—namely, how it came to be that 'adam must procure his livelihood by working the 'adamah, and at that a cursed ground. Thus contrary to the majestic and celebatory message of the first creation account with its affirmed goodness and blessing, the latter account is a dramatic narrative with crisis and resolution in the form of punishment and curse. As professor David Carr astutely observes: in the former, humanity is created in the image and likeness of God and this is declared "good," while in the latter humanity is punished specifically for yearning to be like his god and this is deemed a transgression.[7]

---

7. Carr, *Reading the Fractures of Genesis*, 64. "Gen 1:1—2:3 depicts an omnipotent God creating a godlike humanity. In contrast, Gen 2:4b—3:24 depicts a God who can both fail (Gen 2:19–20) and succeed (Gen 2:21–23). Humanity is not godlike but is created out of earth and punished for acts leading to humanity's being like God (Gen 3:1–24)."

Noteworthy also is the fact that the first creation account emphasizes themes whose purpose and importance may be labeled as liturgical or cultic in nature, such as the importance of the Sabbath (2:3)—thus linking the cultic observance of the Sabbath to the created order of the world—and in general all festivals and rituals governed by the movement of the celestial luminaries, which serve as signs for these "fixed times" (1:14). In fact, there is a heightened emphasis on the correlation between creation and the ritual observance of specific god-created holy days in this creation account (ch. 3). On the contrary, the second creation account displays no concern for these *priestly* matters, and emphasizes its own narrative themes, a sort of anthropological theology interested in such questions as man's relationship to his god, to the ground, obedience, and his lot in life.

All these differences—in theme, style, vocabulary, theology, presentation of the deity, worldview, emphasis, and purpose—and specific contradictions in the order and manner of creation point, irrefutably, to the fact that these two creation accounts were penned by two different authors, for two different purposes, and most likely at two different time periods and for two different audiences. It was only due to a later scribal endeavor that sought to preserve Israel's sacred traditions that these two creation accounts were placed side-by-side as they now appear in their current form.

Now let us take a closer look at each one of these creation accounts individually, being as honest as possible to the texts themselves, and that means attempting to understand them on their terms and from within their own cultural contexts.

GENESIS 1:1—2:3 ON ITS OWN TERMS AND IN ITS OWN HISTORICAL AND LITERARY CONTEXT

Genesis 1:1—2:3's depiction of the creation of the world was shaped by ancient Near Eastern cosmological perspectives and beliefs about the nature of the world and its origins. This fact the text itself bears witness to regardless of the opinions and beliefs of readers living millennia after this text was written. In other words, a thorough, honest, and objective analysis of the text of Genesis 1:1—2:3 on its own terms and as a product of its own cultural and literary world reveals rather convincingly that its creation narrative was shaped by cultural and subjective perspectives, biases, and beliefs about the nature of the world that were unique to the cultures and peoples of the ancient Near East. It is not, in other words, a description of creation from the perspective of a supernatural deity residing outside the cosmos, nor is it inspired by such a point of reference. These are not subjective claims, but the claims that the text itself—our object of study—advances when one reads and understands it on its own terms and from within its own cultural context.

Genesis 1:1–2—Not a Creation *Ex Nihilo*

Despite strong traditional and often authoritative interpretative claims that were formed centuries after this ancient text was written, the opening of Genesis 1 does not depict a *creatio ex nihilo*, that is, a creation out of nothing. The Hebrew text is clear on this point and recognized by all biblical scholars. Rather, what the text of Genesis 1:1–2 informs us is that *when* God began to create, earth—that is, the material substance earth; the Hebrew *'erets* never means the planet Earth (see below)—already existed as a desolate, formless, uninhabitable waste (a *tohu wabohu* in Hebrew) in the midst of a dark surging watery abyss (*tehom*). This is the initial primordial state of creation that the creator deity inherits so to speak, and it is a prominent cultural feature in other ancient Near Eastern creation myths from Egypt to Mesopotamia.

Moreover, as we shall see below, there are specific theological reasons why the author of Genesis 1 composed a creation account where the creator deity creates dry, habitable, life-supporting earth (vv. 9–10) from this primordial, unformed, and desolate earth mass. And these reasons were also shaped by this author's cultural and literary contexts, as well as by the specific historical circumstances in which this author and his audience found themselves. And our author's theological argument—*his message*—should not go ignored or interpreted away simply because it does not conform to modern beliefs and views about the nature of the world and its origins. Rather, our task is to be honest to this ancient text by faithfully reproducing its author's beliefs and worldview—not manipulating them in order to affirm the beliefs and worldview of later readers.

Both creation accounts in the book of Genesis not only belong to the larger cultural world of the ancient Near East that produced them, but they are also part and parcel to a specific literary genre that was widely disseminated throughout this ancient landscape. In other words, the creation accounts of Genesis 1:1—2:3 and 2:4b–24 display the influences of older Near Eastern literary traditions, beliefs, and perspectives about the origins of the sky, earth, and mankind. This knowledge was revealed to us in part through the archaeological discoveries of the late nineteenth century.

In the latter half of the nineteenth century, archaeologists digging around the ancient site of Nineveh, the capital of the Assyrian empire, found the literary remains of Ashurbanipal's library. The Assyrian king, who reigned from 668 to 627 BCE, was somewhat of an antiquarian; he had his scribes collect and copy any existing texts that could be found. The tablets discovered at Nineveh in the latter half of the nineteenth century were the remains of Ashurbanipal's library and contained copies of much earlier Babylonian texts, going as far back as 2000 BCE! What startled linguists working on these cuneiform tablets in the 1870s was the mention of a great flood, a creation, and other similar themes and stories that were present in the narratives of Genesis 1–11. For the first time, scholars and theologians alike realized that stories such as the flood, creation, an original mythic paradise with a primordial pair and a tree of life were not unique to the Bible but were in fact part and parcel to a larger literary and cultural matrix from which the biblical authors freely drew.

Up until this discovery, in other words, it was commonplace among theologians to regard the creation account(s) of Genesis as unique, divinely inspired, and in more fundamentalist circles even historical. With the discovery of other creation myths, however, informed readers were now able to see that the creation accounts in the book of Genesis belonged to a larger literary matrix, whose ideas and perspectives about the nature of the world and its origins were shared throughout the ancient Mediterranean world.

The old Babylonian creation account the *Enuma Elish*, for example, which predates the Genesis accounts by at least a millennium, exhibits many parallels, both structurally and thematically, to the younger creation account of Genesis 1:1—2:3. Even noting its highly mythological content and polytheistic nature, the Babylonian *Enuma Elish* narrates the creation of the sky, earth, and mankind in similar terms to those of Genesis 1:1—2:3, and in the same order. For example, in the older Babylonian creation account the creator deity initially subdues and conquers an original state of watery chaos personified as the goddess Tiamat, and then proceeds to divide her in two, that is, separate the primordial waters into the waters above and the waters below. These waters are then kept apart by the creation of a firmament or the sky, effectively separating the waters above from the waters below. Next, the abode of the gods are attributed to the heavens together with the creation of the luminaries, stars, sun, and moon, to divide the years into months and days—indeed to create our seven-day week. The creation of the earth, that is, dry habitable land, from the waters below then occurs, and finally mankind is created. Lastly, like the ending of Genesis 1:1—2:3, the *Enuma Elish* also ends by assigning rest for the god(s), and both speak of a divine council of some sort (Gen 1:26).

Biblical scholars now realize that this older mythic narrative must have served as a template for the author of Genesis 1:1—2:3, the Priestly writer (ch. 2). In other words, Genesis 1:1—2:3 was not a free composition of its author. This author obviously had literary precursors, one of which was the old Babylonian creation account the *Enuma Elish*, which the Israelites would have come into direct contact with during their captivity in Babylon in the sixth century BCE.

It needs to be stressed that it was less the direct influence of an older text that shaped the ideas and beliefs of the creation account in Genesis 1, and more so the worldview and beliefs of a shared cultural heritage that extended throughout the larger Mediterranean basin. The similarities between the *Enuma Elish* and Genesis 1:1—2:3 represent shared cultural perspectives and beliefs about the nature of the world and its origin. Israelite scribes inherited these cultural perspectives and beliefs, adopted them, and freely modified them to suit their own purposes and monotheistic religious convictions. Many of the ideas and beliefs about the origin of the world expressed above in the *Enuma Elish*, and, as we shall see, similarly in the creation account of Genesis 1:1—2:3, were also present in other creation myths from the ancient Near East. Nearly every surviving creation account from Egypt, for example, presents an original preexisting state of darkness, watery chaos, and a yet unformed landmass prior to creation. This is especially so in the case of the Egyptian cosmogony from Hermopolis, whose primordial state prior to creation is nearly identical to that presented in Genesis 1:2. Personified as preexisting gods, this particular cosmogony speaks of a primeval darkness, a primordial formless earth mass, and the primordial surging waters, through whose separation the earth and heavens were formed and named. Additionally, many of these Egyptian creation myths speak of the primeval waters as the "father of the gods" and depict creation as the emergence of habitable earth from these chaotic waters, similar to what we find in Genesis 1:9–10.

Thus, one of the ideas that the author of Genesis 1 inherited from his larger cultural and literary world about the nature of his world and its origins was that the creation of the earth and the skies, of ordered life in general, was the result of separating light from primordial darkness (1:4), of separating a primordial surging water mass (*tehom*) into the waters above and the waters below (1:6–7) to form a space in their midst (1:7), wherein the skies were named (1:8) and the luminaries by which the cosmos progressed in an orderly fashion were created (1:14), and finally by forming habitable land from a primordial formless and empty (*tohu wabohu*) earth mass and separating it out from the waters below and naming it "earth" (1:10).[8]

In general terms, then, the authors and cultures of these ancient Near Eastern creation myths, Genesis 1 included, did not conceive of creation as an act of creating matter, but as an act of creating order, form, purpose, and habitable land with tamed and separated waters out of an initial primeval state of untamed waters, darkness, and an unformed and uninhabitable earth mass. Whether speaking of the Babylonian *Enuma Elish*, Egyptian cosmogonies, or Genesis 1, the emphasis falls on presenting the creation of a habitable orderly world from an initial state of formlessness, darkness, and untamed waters, through the creator deity's act of separating this initial primordial matter, assigning functions or setting boundaries to the separated elements, and naming or calling into existence each component of the world as it was perceived by the peoples and cultures of the ancient Near East. The idea of the creation of matter out of nothing was simply not a perspective adopted by the cultures of the ancient Near East, the Israelites included. The closest thing we have to the idea of creation out of nothing are a couple of Egyptian creation myths that pose a single creator deity as the origin of life, and from whose body, sky, earth, and water emerge. In other words, the idea that the world originated through the creation of matter from nothing simply did not exist. Such an idea would not only have

8. The two creation accounts that open the book of Genesis are not the only creation stories found in this corpus of literature we now call the Bible. A much older mythic tale is preserved in passages from the Psalms (Ps 74:13–17; 89:9–13; 104:5–13), the book of Job (26:12–13; 38:4–11), and the Prophets. These passages directly reference or allude to a more archaic Near Eastern myth—a myth which describes the creation of the heavens and the earth in terms of the creator deity, in the biblical sources Yahweh, slaying a primeval sea monster variously represented as Leviathan or Rahab, from whose body the sky and the earth are created. The theme of Yahweh battling a primordial serpent that leads to the serpent's destruction and the creation of the sky and earth from its slain body is a common mythic feature found in many of Israel's ancient Near Eastern neighbors. In the *Enuma Elish* cited above, the goddess Tiamat, who is represented as a water serpent, is slain by the god Marduk and it is from her slain body that the sky and the earth are created. Yahweh's slaying of the mythic Leviathan or Rahab belongs to this same literary tradition.

been inconceivable to the peoples and cultures of this ancient landscape, but inferior to the views they did hold about the creation of the habitable world.

That is to say, our ancient Near Eastern forerunners, the biblical scribes included, deemed that the creation of an orderly world, of habitable land with tamed and separated seas and a heaven that provided light, order, and signs for the measurement of days, months, years, and even holy festivals from an initial state of darkness, untamed waters, and unformed earth was a more powerful statement to make about the creator deity. More significantly, the act of creating order from disorder, light from darkness, form from formlessness answered the specific concerns ancient peoples of the Near East had living in, as they perceived it, a hostile world with forces that regularly needed to be controlled. So presenting a creator deity who could, and did in fact, tame the forces of nature, subdue darkness, control the seas, create life from barrenness, form from formlessness was a direct result of how the ancients perceived the world they lived in and the forces that acted upon it. This was the message behind such creation stories. The creator deity had full control over the destructive forces that continually threatened life, order, and the goodness of the created world. Most significantly, as we shall see below, the ability of Yahweh to subdue chaos, form light from darkness, create fertile and habitable earth from a formless uninhabitable earth mass also had a very significant and immediate meaning to the historical audience for whom Genesis 1:1—2:3 was composed.

Besides these culturally shared beliefs about the nature of the world and its origins and the literary heritage that the author of Genesis 1 inherited, there are sound textual data that support the idea that our biblical scribe did not compose a creation account depicting the creator deity creating the earth and the skies out of nothing. For the text itself clearly makes the opposite claim.

First, as many Hebraists have noted, Genesis 1:1 opens with a temporal clause. This is a complex grammatical topic, but simplified, the way in which Genesis' first word is constructed—a preposition (*be-*) plus a noun (*re'shit*)—places the word in the construct state, that is, a noun which is followed by another noun in an "of" relationship.[9] Thus a literal translation of Genesis' first word, *bere'shit*, is properly "in the beginning *of*." And this is exactly what we find as the proper understanding of *bere'shit* when this same word appears elsewhere in the Hebrew Bible. So, for example, the

9. Smith, *Priestly Vision*, 44.

Hebrew of Jeremiah 27:1, *bere'shit mamlekhet yehoyaqim*, is properly trans-lated: "In the beginning *of* the kingdom of Jehoiakim." But the grammatical problem in Genesis 1:1 is that *bere'shit* is not followed by a noun but rather a verb-subject pair: *bere'shit bara' 'elohim*. Thus a literal rendering of the first three words of Genesis is impossible: "In the beginning *of* God created." In other words, according to the construct state of Genesis' opening word (*bere'shit*), this verb-subject pair grammatically needs to be understood in an "of" relationship to *bere'shit*. This is why many modern translations have sought to capture the temporal aspect in the opening word of the book of Genesis by rendering the Hebrew more accurately as: "In the beginning of God's creating . . ." or "In the beginning when God created . . ." or even "When God began to create . . ."

The idea that creation narratives commenced with a temporal clause that indicated when the creator deity began his creative act is also attested in other ancient Near Eastern creation myths. The *Enuma Elish* opens with a temporal clause which doubles as the text's title: "*When* on high the heav-ens had not yet been named, nor earth below pronounced by name . . ." Likewise, Genesis' second creation account also begins with a temporal clause: "*In the day when* god Yahweh made earth and skies . . ." (2:4b).

Another interesting parallel between the *Enuma Elish*'s opening state-ment and that of Genesis 1:1 is the reference to an earth that has not yet been named—that is, not yet been created or called into existence. The rhe-torical problem is: by what name do you call the primordial matter before that matter is named and created as earth proper? Although using the word "earth," the *Enuma Elish* responds by alluding to the primordial matter that *will become* earth: "when earth was not yet named." Genesis 1:1 similarly reproduces this idea but employs a different literary technique: referencing the earth that will be (1:9) as initially *tohu wabohu*, without form and void (1:2). What is implied might be rendered: "In the beginning when God created the skies and the earth, and *that which would become* earth was without form and void . . ." And indeed this reading is supported by the text itself when in vv. 9–10 dry habitable land is created and named "earth" for the first time. So if earth proper, that is, dry habitable land, is not created nor named until the third day, then what existed prior to earth's creation must have been none other than a formless, nameless mass of desolate "earth" for lack of a better word. Earth, then, has a very specific meaning in this creation narrative. It is dry, habitable, life-bearing land (v. 10). And this, our text informs us, was created from a preexisting formless waste of non-life-supporting matter or "earth" (v. 2).

This is the proper message conveyed in Genesis 1:1–10 (detailed below), and it depicts the creator deity in his most powerful and omnipotent role—creating form and life-bearing earth with tamed and separated seas by subduing, separating, and setting life-supporting boundaries to an initial formless mass of desolate "earth" and chaotic waters. This is how the ancient Israelites perceived their world and its origins, not out of nothing—a statement that would have been vacuous to them—but rather through the subduing of the forces of the seas, of destruction, of chaos, of barrenness, etc. Thus similar to the *Enuma Elish*, Genesis 1:1–2 must also be seen as a temporal clause doubling as the text's title: "In the beginning when God created the skies and the earth, and the [yet to be created and named] earth was formless and desolate . . ."

Thus not only is the idea of preexistent matter part and parcel to the mindset and worldview of the ancient Near East, but the syntax and grammar of Genesis' opening sentence, like other creation myths of the ancient Near East, strongly support the fact that the Israelites also depicted their creator deity in a role of subduing, separating, and creating the very elements of the world from a preexistent state of formless, desolate matter.

Second, the precise function of the verb *bara'* highlights the creative act as one of separating. There are three verbs used in the two creation accounts in Genesis to speak of making or creating: *bara'*, "to create"; *'asah*, "to make"; and *yatsar*, "to form." The verb *bara'*, at least in the context of Genesis 1, connotes the act of creating by means of separating out, or distinguishing. The skies and the earth, we are told, only come into existence by separating them out from preexistent matter, by setting their boundaries, and by naming them. Thus, it is not until v. 9 that earth, that is dry land, is created at the moment it is separated out and distinguished from the waters below, and thenceforth named: "And God called the land 'earth'" (1:10). Likewise, the skies (*shamayim*), that is, the waters above, only come into existence through an act of separating, subduing, and partitioning them off from the waters below, both of which were originally part of the primordial deep (*tehom*). What is therefore implied in Genesis' opening statement is that the skies and the earth came into existence through a creative act of separating them out from preexisting matter—exactly how many Egyptian cosmogonies also begin.

Third and most significantly is the fact that the text itself explicitly asserts that neither the skies nor the earth were created *ex nihilo*! For the text, and more so the message of its author, clearly depict the creation of earth proper from a desolate and void (*tohu wabohu*) yet to be named "earth," and the skies from an original watery chaos (*tehom*). That is, both the creation of the skies in vv. 6–8 and the creation of the earth in vv. 9–10 do not occur from nothing!

Per our text, earth proper is "dry land," the material life-supporting substance earth, which does not get created until vv. 9–10, when the creator deity himself calls it into existence through an act of separating, defining, and naming it. Furthermore, it is not created out of nothing. For again, per our text, this earth which only comes into existence in vv. 9–10 was created from an initial formless, undefined, and desolate "earth" mass that was originally submerged in the surging deep (1:2). Why this author explicitly presents the creation of earth from an initial state of *tohu wabohu* is addressed below. In any event, the text is quite clear: the earth that only comes into existence in vv. 9–10 was not created *ex nihilo*. It was created from this initial unformed and barren "earth" mass.

Much of the confusion, or plain inaccuracy, behind modern claims of the earth's creation out of nothing not only arise from a misunderstanding of Genesis 1:2 and a lack of knowledge about its author's culturally conditioned beliefs and worldview, but also in thinking that the Hebrew word for earth (*'erets*) means the planet Earth. The text and its cultural context nowhere support this modern assumption. Rather, what is created is life-bearing land (vv. 9–10), the earth beneath one's feet, created from desolate, undefined, and yet to be named "earth" (v. 2). So to be honest about our ancient text and the message of its author, there is no creation of the planet Earth imagined here. Such an idea would have been inconceivable per our author's culturally conditioned perceptions and knowledge about his world, or in this case lack thereof (treated more fully below).

Likewise, neither the text nor its author presents the creation of the skies out of nothing. For what is to become the skies or the heavens (*shamayim*) is the *raqi'a*, which God creates in order to separate the initial primordial teeming waters into the waters above and the waters below. I suppose one could argue that the text does present the creator deity making this *raqi'a* out of nothing (1:7), but not in the sense that there was nothing preexistent prior to its creation. For again the text clearly states that this *raqi'a*, which was conceptualized by the ancient Israelites as a solid transparent barrier holding back the waters above, was created as a tool for the deity to separate and keep separate these initial primordial waters, half of which are now held above this barrier (see below). It is this barrier or *raqi'a* that gets named "the skies" (v. 8), and its primary function was to keep back the waters above.

Finally, a grave theological problem is unavoidably created when one wrongly imposes later theological claims of *creatio ex nihilo* onto the text of Genesis 1:1–10—a text which clearly states otherwise. Since the creation of earth in vv. 9–10 happens through the shaping and naming of an initial formless preexisting "earth mass," and the creation of the skies in vv. 6–8 happens as a direct result of subduing and dividing the primordial untamed waters, then in imposing a later and erroneous theological assertion of *creatio ex nihilo* one is forced to conclude, since the text *does not* present the creation of *shamayim* out of nothing nor the creation of *'erets* out of nothing, that the creator deity was unable to do so! This is absurd, yet unavoidable if we follow this line of erroneous thinking to its end. For, if it was the deity's original intention to create the skies and the earth out of nothing—or let's put this more accurately—*if it was the original intention of the biblical scribe to present his god* creating the skies and the earth out of nothing, then why did he not do this?

In other words, in imposing later theological assertions of creation from nothing onto this ancient text what you end up with as the creator deity's supposed first act of creating matter out of nothing is the creation of formless, meaningless, lifeless, and desolate earth covered by a surging watery abyss surrounded in bleak darkness—all of which then needed to be re-created! Not a flattering portrait of a creator deity, and certainly not what our author intended! This is just one example of the violence done to these ancient texts and to the beliefs of their authors when later readers force their own beliefs and views onto these texts. According to this forced modern reading, the conclusion that must be drawn is that the creator deity could not do what he intended to do on his first go: the earth and skies proper needed to be created a second time from the matter that this deity supposedly created in v. 2! This translates to presenting a creator deity that textually didn't, and theologically couldn't, create the earth (v. 10) and the skies (v. 8) *ex nihilo*! An absurd conclusion drawn when one erroneously imposes modern assertions onto an ancient text whose real message is ignored, neglected, or interpreted away.

Last but certainly not least, as mentioned earlier the composition of a creation account displaying a deity that could transform formless and desolate earth (*tohu wabohu*) into habitable life-bearing land had a direct significance for the audience of Genesis 1:1—2:3. It's time we took a look at this.

Before God commences the act of creating the habitable world, the author of Genesis 1 informs us that what was to become earth existed in a state of formlessness and desolation—a *tohu wabohu* in Hebrew. This image was not only shaped by the ideas and beliefs shared throughout the ancient Near Eastern world, but it was equally influenced by the specific historical circumstance of the author and his audience—at least how he and his audience perceived it. The rare Hebrew expression *tohu wabohu* or *tohu* alone and the image it invoked were unique to the literature of the sixth century BCE. That is we only find this image and this vocabulary in other texts from the postexilic era, and specifically to depict the historical crisis so often alluded to in these texts.[10] Paying attention to these textual details allows us to see more clearly what the author of Genesis 1:1—2:3 hoped to convey through his creation account, and more importantly to whom!

In the aftermath of the destruction of Judah by the Babylonians in the earlier sixth century BCE and the desolation of its land and the turning of fruitful fields into wildernesses, the author of Jeremiah professes: "I looked on the earth and behold it was formless and desolate (*tohu wabohu*), and to the skies and they had no light" (Jer 4:23). The image put forth here is remarkably similar to that of Genesis 1:2: the earth is depicted in a state of formlessness and desolation, a *tohu wabohu*. Is this then a vision of the primordial state of creation as depicted in Genesis 1:2? Not quite. Although the author does borrow this same image, here used to express decreation, it is used here to depict the harsh realities and outcome of the Babylonian destruction of the land of Judah and its people in 587 BCE. In other words, the language and image that Jeremiah and other exilic writers of the sixth century used to portray the utter annihilation of the land of Judah at the hands of the Babylonians, who decimated its land, burned Jerusalem and Yahweh's temple to the ground, and left the land barren and covered in ashes, was the same language and imagery used to describe the preexistent state of creation—*tohu wabohu*.

In fact, references to Judah specifically, and the earth in general, as a *tohu wabohu*, a wasteland, a barren, sterile, and desolate wilderness, were

---

10. These insights indebted to Smith, *Priestly Vision*, 57–58.

typical postexilic descriptions of the aftermath of the Babylonian destruction as they laid siege to the land and utterly destroyed and burnt everything they encountered, from cities to fields. Thus in another text from the prophetic traditions of the sixth century BCE, the author of Deutero-Isaiah, attempting to console the exilic community, has Yahweh utter these words:

> For thus saith Yahweh, he who created (*bara'*) the skies, the very god who formed (*yatsar*) the earth and made (*'asah*) it; he himself established it. He did not create (*bara'*) it a desolation (*tohu*), but formed (*yatsar*) it to be habitable. (Isa 45:18)

The allusion to (re)creation is more apparent here than in Jeremiah's text. At core it is a message of hope to the postexilic community that Yahweh will turn Judah from a *tohu wabohu*—that is, the wasteland left after the Babylonian destruction—back into habitable life-bearing earth. More instructively, our author professes that Yahweh did not create the earth a *tohu*. This too speaks against modern attempts to claim that Genesis 1:2 depicts God creating *ex nihilo* earth as a *tohu wabohu*. But as we saw, both Genesis 1:1–10 and now Isaiah 45:18 speak against these modern interpretive claims.

The point that I'm trying to make is that this specific vocabulary and imagery are unique to the exilic and postexilic literature of the sixth century BCE and reflect these authors' reality, or at least how they perceived their reality—as a desolation, a wasteland. In like manner, the author of Genesis 1 is also expressing the same idea in his creation account, and to the same audience and for the same purpose! In this case, the *tohu wabohu* of Genesis 1:2 serves a dual purpose: on the worldly level it describes the primordial desolate and formless "earth" which the creator deity eventually forms into habitable life-bearing land; and on the historic plane it describes the state of desolation and waste wrought by the Babylonian aftermath of 587 BCE. If this is so, then the Priestly creation account, like the Isaiah passage above, is an expression of the very hopes and reality of an exilic and/or postexilic community and how this community perceived its own condition. That is to say, the author of Genesis 1 purposely composed his creation narrative to portray the creator deity creating habitable earth from a desolate formless void (a *tohu wabohu*) in order to console his sixth-century audience who saw themselves living upon desolate, barren, and uninhabitable land. It is meant as an affirmative message: that as God *had* created a habitable earth from a preexistent formless waste (*tohu wabohu*), so too he can, *and will*, reestablish the land of Judah as habitable from its current condition of desolation and barrenness: "He did not create it a desolation (*tohu*), but formed it to be habitable." The message and image reaffirm to this exilic community the goodness and holiness in the created order of the world despite their current plight living in *tohu*. This is why creation from nothing meant nothing. What the Israelites sought to portray was a deity powerful enough to make—to transform—a desolate, formless, barren wasteland into fertile, habitable, life-sustaining earth, as was necessitated after the Babylonian destruction of Judah in 587 BCE. Both Genesis 1:1–10 and these passages from the prophetic tradition accomplish this, and I might add marvelously well.

My central aim here was not to argue that Genesis 1:1–2 does not portray a creation out of nothing, which is certainly the case, but rather to demonstrate that the biblical scribe's presentation of the origins of creation from a primordial watery chaos with unformed, desolate earth was shaped by the ideas and beliefs shared throughout the ancient world, and that the description of creation in Genesis 1:1–2 is a culturally dependent account shaped from the perspectives, beliefs, and ideas about the nature of the world shared throughout the ancient Mediterranean basin.

Modern readers who are ignorant of the literary and historical contexts of the Bible's ancient texts—literary contexts that the biblical scribes themselves were well aware of and consciously drew from—but nonetheless feel qualified to pontificate on the meaning of these ancient documents are just being disingenuous to these texts and the beliefs and views of their authors. Not only that, but this type of practice—pontificating meaning on an ancient text while willfully being ignorant of the cultural and literary contexts, beliefs, and worldviews advocated in the text itself—has the adverse effect of merely fueling more ignorance and in turn generating staunch hypocritical views, since one now believes, out of ignorance, something about the text which the text in fact does not claim! Again, our goal is to be honest to the texts *on their terms* and to the beliefs and worldviews of their authors, even, and especially, if that means acknowledging that our culture's views and beliefs about these texts are inaccurate.

Genesis 1:3–5—Day Is Light

Modern readers often express their perplexity at the fact that Genesis 1:3 presents the creation of light before the creation of the luminary that produces light, the sun, whose creation does not happen until day 4 (1:16). How can light be created or exist, it is often asked, before the sun was created?

The problem with this and similar questions is that they impose our knowledge about the cosmos, indeed an objective understanding about the workings of our solar system, onto this ancient text whose culture did not possess this type of knowledge. We know that the sun is the source of light for our solar system. But the ancient cultures and peoples that produced this creation account did not possess this knowledge and apparently held different ideas about the nature of their world. This fact the text itself bears witness to.

In other words, Genesis' portrait of the creation of the world was not shaped by objective, scientific, or divinely-inspired knowledge about the world; rather, it was shaped by the perspectives, beliefs, and limited empirical understanding—or misunderstanding as the case may be—of the nature of the world and its workings as ancient man perceived it. Our goal should not be to impose modern truths onto this ancient document, nor attempt to harmonize the text with our modern scientific knowledge about the world. Rather, our task is to understand the text on *its terms* and as a product of its own unique cultural perspectives, and to be able to reproduce this understanding as faithfully and honestly as possible. We should allow the text to invite us into its ancient worldview and belief system, not impose ours onto the text.

Having said that, it would initially appear that the Israelite scribe who penned Genesis 1, and the larger cultural perspective from which he drew, did not see or understand the sun as the source of light, that is, the source of day or daylight. Indeed, as expressed in Genesis 1:15, the sun was understood as a light-emitting source, as was mistakenly the moon. But it appears that it was not seen as the source of daylight. The sun and the moon were created "to distinguish between the day and the night" not as the sources for day and night. This is a radically different idea from what we in fact know to be true. What was this author attempting to convey then?

There are basically three things that happen in Genesis 1:3–5. Following what our biblical author has presented so far in his composition of the creation of the world, we see that to this primeval state of darkness that spread out over an untamed watery abyss which covered a formless, vacuous piece of earth (1:2), light was added. "And God said, 'Let there be light!'" Darkness need not have been created since it already existed.

Second, the text informs us that God separates this newly created light from the primeval darkness, and lastly calls or identifies this light as "day," and conversely darkness as "night." "And there was evening and there was morning—one day."

So over this watery untamed abyss of formless earth, alternating sequences of day and night now exist. This is significant because what the text presents the deity creating first is the day or daylight. In other words, the light that comes into existence is not called "the sun" but rather "day." Day was essentially conceived of as light, as being composed of light. According to our ancient scribe, day by its very nature *is* light! Ancient peoples might have deduced this from the observation that even when the sun doesn't appear or is hidden behind clouds, it is still daylight out. Thus, the separation and alternation between day and night, light and darkness, are set by an initial act of the creator deity and not by the sun. This is our author's argument.

This idea is reinforced elsewhere in the text. There are only three places in Genesis 1 where God is presented creating something or calling it into existence and then immediately naming it. It's instructive to look at these three occurrences together: (1) light is created and called "day"; (2) the firmament or domed expanse is created and called "the skies"; and (3) dry land is created or simply commanded to appear and is called "earth." We notice that the name given to each of these elements expresses what it inherently or essentially is. What is earth? It is dry land. What is the sky? It is the domed expanse (*raqiʿa*) which God created to separate the waters below from those above. And finally, what is day? It is light. In other words our ancient author perceived day as essentially equivalent to light. So the source of day's light, or daylight, was not seen as the sun, but rather as the very essence of day itself, as God created it to be is our author's point. This is very instructive for a proper understanding of how ancient Israelites viewed their world. Light, or more appropriately day, exists because God created it. The two are one and the same: as dry land is earth, and the domed expanse above is the sky, so too light *is* day.

The fact that this author presents the creation of day as the deity's first creative act is not a coincidence. Certainly it immediately lends itself to the thematic and structural framework of what follows—five more days of creation and a seventh day of rest, where each day is a successive pattern of evening and morning. It must additionally be borne in mind that, contrary to our modern knowledge of the workings of the cosmos, the successive coming and going of evening and morning, night and day, were not defined by the appearance and disappearance of the sun; rather, as has already been demonstrated, and according to our author's limited knowledge and culturally shaped beliefs, night and day, darkness and light, were separated and distinguished "elements" or spheres created by God himself. Thus as we previously saw in the case of Genesis 1:1–2, the author's subjective and culturally defined perspectives and beliefs about the nature of his world are transferred to the god of his text, and this god is then presented creating the subjective world that our author perceived and experienced!

Second, the creation of day as God's first act serves a larger purpose, one that has an immediate significance for this particular author and the priestly guild he represented (ch. 2). The fact that this author composed a creation account that revolved around days, that is, a creation account that embeds a calendar system directly into the creation of the world, is extremely significant. In essence, this priestly author has just presented us with an argument that declares that the calendar system, Sabbath, and Yahweh's sacred festivals (i.e., "the fixed times" of 1:14) were all built into the very fabric of the cosmos by God at creation! The nonobservance of any of these god-created holy days, therefore, was inexcusable as we shall see (ch. 3).

Genesis 1:6–8—Life inside a Water Bubble

When ancient man looked up at the sky, what he perceived was akin to what he observed when looking out over the seas—an expanse of crystal-clear blue water. This observation was confirmed of course by the very fact that it rained. For where else did rain come from if not from the waters above the sky?

Similarly, when ancient Mediterranean peoples looked toward the horizon, what they saw was that the waters above eventually came into contact with the waters of the seas, that both the blue waters above and the blue waters below touched each other at the horizons. Thus, it was observed that the waters above, that is, the sky, had its starting point at the horizon where it came into contact with the waters below, and then arched far above like a dome and descended again to meet the waters below on the opposite horizon. According to these limited empirical observations then, ancient Mediterranean man, Israelites included, perceived their world as surrounded by two vast bodies of water, those above and those below, and that those waters which arched high above them like a dome were somehow held in place. This was the world which the ancient Israelites perceived and lived in. It was therefore only natural to ponder questions about its origin: How did the waters get above the sky and what holds them up there? How did they obtain their current domed shape? Where did they originate from? And what about the waters below? In short, how did *this* world come to be?

Genesis 1:6–8 was specifically written to answer these questions. In other words, what the god of this text is portrayed creating is the world as it was perceived and culturally defined by ancient Israelite scribes, the world which *they saw* from their limited empirical observations, not the world as it actually is! This fact the text itself bears witness to.

As we have already seen in our examination of Genesis 1:1–2 and 1:3–5, the same applies here: Genesis 1:6–8 is a subjective description and explanation from the viewpoint of its author and his culture of how the world *as he perceived it*, with its waters above and waters below, came into existence. It is a bottoms up approach. The author's perspectives and culturally defined beliefs about the nature of his world are transferred to the god of his text who then creates the subjective world that this very author and his culture perceived and lived in. It is a creation account that matches its author's culturally conditioned "truths" as it were about the world. Thus we must be careful not to impose our understanding and knowledge of the world onto *his* text, nor try to conform his beliefs to ours. Rather we ought to strive to be honest to this ancient document and the beliefs and views of its author.

After creating daylight and separating it from primeval darkness, now night, our author then presents God taming and separating the primeval waters. "And God said, 'Let there be a domed expanse (*raqiʻa*)[11] in

---

11. My translation of *raqiʻa* as "a solid domed expanse" may seem alarming at first, but it is the clearest image available for expressing what the Hebrew invokes. The verb form of *raqiʻa* means "to beat out" or "to hammer out" and is attested with respect to hammering out metal plates or bowls (e.g., Exod 39:3; Jer 10:9), thus a domed or concaved shape. More specifically the verb *raqaʻ* is used in Job 37:18 to speak of Yahweh *"hammering out thinly* the firmament, hard like the reflective surface of poured metal." And Psalm 19 further supports the idea that the *raqiʻa* was seen as a manifestation of Yahweh's handiwork or craftsmanship (19:1). We should further note that both Genesis 1:6–8's use of *raqiʻa* and Job 37:18's use of *raqaʻ* conceptualize the sky as a hard or solid thinly hammered out metallic-like domed surface, likened to the reflective substance of poured metal. Other references to the domed shaped *raqiʻa* or sky occur in Isa 40:22 and Job 22:14, as well as Deut 4:32 and Prov 8:27–28 which both envision the skies touching

the center of the waters and let it separate the waters from the waters'"
(Gen 1:6).

Once gain, the reason why the primordial waters *needed* to be separated is best explained by realizing that our author is working backwards,
from what he perceives and has been culturally conditioned to believe
about the nature of his world to the composition of a creation narrative
that then explains the origins of the elements of his world *as he perceived
it* through his culturally conditioned perspectives and beliefs. So Genesis
1:1–10 is not an account of the creation of the world in objective, scientific
terms. Rather it is an account of the creation *of a perception of the world* as
envisioned by ancient man. Since the ancient Israelites perceived and believed that there existed a vast body of water above the sky, held in check
by the sky itself, our author therefore creates a narrative that explains the
origin of these waters above the sky. In the end, the text legitimates the
author's culturally defined worldview by having God create it!

Thus in accord with his perceptions and beliefs about the world, our
author presents God making (*'asah*) this solid domed expanse (*raqi'a*)
in the middle of the primordial waters (*mayim*) in order to separate out
the waters which are now above it from the waters now below it, effectively conforming to our Israelite scribe's perception of his world. Finally,
the text informs us: "And God called this domed expanse (*raqi'a*) 'skies'
(*shamayim*). And there was evening and there was morning—a second
day" (Gen 1:8).

Since the Hebrew word for "skies" (*shamayim*) is composed of
the letter *shin* plus the word for water, *mayim*—always in the plural,

---

the earth on each end. In addition to these, there are other biblical passages that also attempt to describe this *raqi'a*. In Ezekiel 1:22, for example, the *raqi'a* is described "like the
sight of awe-inspiring crystal" or perhaps ice, and is strong enough to support Yahweh's
throne which rests upon it (Ezek 10:1; Exod 24:10). Likewise in Exodus 24:10 this *raqi'a*
is described "like a smooth-paved work of sapphire, and like the substance of the skies in
regard to brightness." And in Job 37:18, as we have already noted, it is spoken of as looking like a poured metallic mirror of some sort. All of these textual traditions support the
view that the Israelites conceptualized the sky—that is the *raqi'a* of Genesis 1—as a solid
crystal or metallic-like domed expanse of a sapphire hue, no doubt reflecting the color of
the waters above which this solid crystalline domed expanse supported. Additionally, the
primeval waters are depicted as occupying the space above this *raqi'a* or sky elsewhere in
the Bible (e.g., Ps 148:4), and it was because of this solid barrier's openings that the waters
above pour down and flood the earth in the Priestly writer's flood narrative (see Gen
7:11; 8:2). Indeed, rain, snow, and hail were all believed to be kept in storehouses above
the *raqi'a* which had "windows" to allow them in. And the birds of Gen 1:20 are said to
fly in front of the *raqi'a* in the open air, not in this solid domed expanse.

"waters"—it is quite possible that what came to be called the skies was a combination of the solid domed expanse or *raqiʿa* and the waters above it. For we are informed in v. 14 that the *raqiʿa*, where the luminaries are to be set, was part of the skies or *shamayim*: "let there be lights in the domed expanse *of the skies.*" And likewise in v. 20 we are informed that the birds are to fly in front of the domed expanse of the skies. If the skies are both the solid domed expanse and the waters above, which seems to be what is implied here, then the skies (*shamayim*) are nothing more than half of the untamed preexisting waters (*mayim*) and the crystalline-like domed expanse (*raqiʿa*), which now holds back these same waters.

Thus once again we observe that the creation account in Genesis 1 does not represent some scientific, objective, or divinely inspired account of the origins of the material world, but rather the creation of a world as perceived by ancient Israelites. It was precisely from these subjective, culturally conditioned beliefs that biblical scribes then proceeded to compose creation myths whose aim was to explain *their* observable world. In this instance, how did the waters above come to be formed and held in check? Genesis 1:1–8 responds by claiming that they were created through an act of separating them out from the initial watery abyss (*tehom*), and holding them above the sky through the creation of a solid domed expanse.

Finally, and again, the argument that our ancient Israelite scribe was interested in presenting was not where matter originated. Threatened on all sides, above and below, by the primordial waters, the Israelite scribe painted a portrait not of a creator deity who creates matter out of nothing, but of a creator deity who creates ordered life by (continuously) subduing, taming, and controlling the primordial forces and elements that existed prior to his creative act, and which still exert their force in the world. It is a creation that is forever being re-created as it were, that is, forever keeping at bay the primordial waters above and below.

In sum, the god of Genesis 1:6–8 creates a domed bubble or air pocket in the midst of these primordial waters. According to the text, then, God creates a finite space in the midst of, and encased from all sides by, these primeval waters. This is not some outlandish theological claim that I am making. Rather, as a biblical scholar I'm reproducing the claims of the text—a text which reveals the culturally defined beliefs, attitudes, and worldview of the ancient people that penned it.

Genesis 1:9–10—The Creation of the Material Substance Earth, Not the Planet

We are so habituated by what the English word "earth" means to us in our scientific postmodern world that we seldom stop to ask if that's the same meaning intended in the Hebrew word 'erets.

> When we read Genesis 1:1, "in the beginning God created the heavens and the earth," we picture the origin of the atmosphere, space, solar systems, and galaxies. We think of the creation of the planet in our solar system named "Earth," whose shape is an oblate spheroid or a rotationally symmetric ellipsoid. This mental picture is natural, because the English term "Earth" is the name of the planet in this solar system on which humans reside. But in Genesis 1 "earth" does not mean the planet Earth. Genesis reports the origin of the "heavens and earth" as such terms meant in the author's time and within his worldview, which did not include a twenty-first century acquaintance with astronomy. What does "earth" mean in Genesis 1? The answer is provided in the text itself.[12]

It is rare to find such an accurately and succinctly put introduction to the textual problem at hand that I had to borrow this one to serve as my own introduction. This is quite shocking since it comes from a theologian in the Wesleyan tradition who has very different beliefs than myself. In fact it could be said we stand at opposite ends of the spectrum.

Nonetheless, this exemplifies something that I have repeatedly voiced here: that biblical scholarship proper is not about the reader's beliefs or non-beliefs, not about finding our beliefs or scientific truths in these ancient documents, but about understanding and faithfully reproducing *their* beliefs. Dr. Winslow and I can agree on the point expressed above, because that the Hebrew 'erets did not and does not signify the planet Earth is a fact borne from reading the text on its own terms and in its own historical and literary contexts, regardless of the beliefs of its readers. This is what I have been advocating as the objective study of the Bible. It is the texts and the culturally conditioned beliefs expressed in them that are the object of our study—and not what later readers believe or are told to believe about these texts.

So then what does 'erets mean according to the ancient Israelite scribe that penned this text? What exactly does he portray God creating?

---

12. Winslow, "Understanding Earth," lines 1–10.

At the end of vv. 6–8 we are left with an image of two parted bodies of water, the waters above and the waters below, in the midst of which is a bowel-shaped pocket of air. This open space was created by the arched barrier (*raqi'a*) which the creator deity made and set in place to keep the waters above from falling and rejoining the waters below (something that actually does happen in this writer's flood narrative).[13] This solid domed expanse is then called "the skies" (*shamayim*), so that in the end it is the sky itself which holds back the waters above, and these waters in return give the sky its blue color.

The text then turns to the waters below the skies. These waters are collected together and subdued to form "seas." It is from this body of water that we are informed dry land (*yabbashah*) appears.

> And God said, "Let the waters under the skies be gathered to one
> place and let the dry land be seen." And it was so. And God called
> the dry land "earth" and he called the collection of waters "seas."
> And God saw that it was good. (Gen 1:9–10)

There are several things to observe in these verses. First, we are informed that from the action of gathering the waters below the skies into tamed bodies of water, which are named "seas," dry land can now emerge from the waters below and be seen. The Hebrew verb here is *ra'ah*, "to see," and it is the same verb used in v. 10 when our author writes, "and God *saw* that it was good." In v. 9, this verb appears in a passive imperative construction: "*let be seen* the dry land"—normally translated as "let the dry land appear." Thus in no manner of speaking does v. 9 speak of the creation *ex nihilo* of earth, which is defined by the text as dry land (*yabbashah*). Rather, dry land *emerges* from the collected waters below; it is commanded to appear, to become visible.

This narrative detail draws us back to v. 2, where yet to be created earth, that is dry land specifically, preexisted in a state of formlessness and desolation (*tohu wabohu*), itself immersed in the surging waters of the primeval deep (*tehom*). Again, it is best to understand "earth" in v. 2 as the material substance earth, which has as of yet not been formed, named, nor

13. This culturally conditioned cosmological perspective of the world is also found in this author's flood story. Contrary to the Yahwist version of the flood story, where it rains for forty days and forty nights (Gen 7:4, 12), in the Priestly version the domed barrier which holds back the waters above is loosened to let those waters retake their original chaotic and untamed position (Gen 7:11; 8:2). It is a true undoing of creation from this author's perspective. For more about the Yahwist and Priestly versions of the Bible's flood stories, see my forthcoming *Understanding Bible Contradictions*.

really created as dry habitable life-supporting land, earth proper. All this happens on day 3 in vv. 9–10. So, the preexisting formless and desolate material substance earth that was submerged in the watery deep of v. 2 only emerges as earth proper, that is, life-sustaining land, after the creator deity has subdued the primeval forces that threaten life—the untamed waters and darkness. This is yet another example of the creator god subduing the primeval elements rather than creating matter out of nothing. The waters recede and are tamed to expose, or create the conditions for, life-supporting dry earth—ʾerets proper.

Thus, far from presenting God creating Earth, a spherical planet orbiting a sun in one of many galaxies in infinite space (none of whose ideas existed to the author of this text), the text of Genesis 1 presents its god forming the substance earth, that is per our text dry, habitable, flat land which now rests on the waters below, and encasing it within a finite area of space, itself enclosed and defined by a solid domed expanse called the sky, which further functioned to hold back the primordial waters above it. In short, what the god of Genesis 1 creates is this:

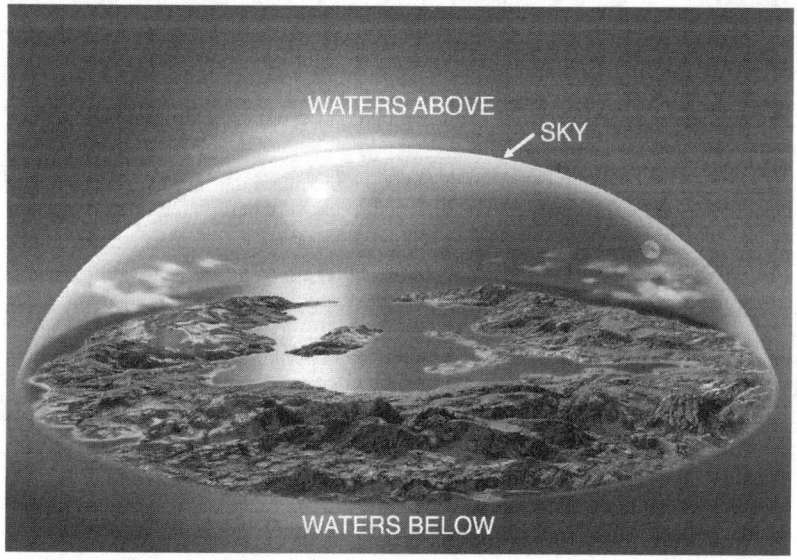

not this!

In other words, our author's presentation and imagination of how God created the material stuff of his world were shaped by his own subjective and culturally defined perceptions and beliefs about his world. These beliefs were deduced from what ancient man (mis)perceived on an empirical level: for example, rain fell from water which existed above the sky; whereas natural springs, deltas, and flooding led to the belief that the earth "floated" on and was supported by waters that existed below the earth, that is, below the dry ground beneath one's feet.[14] These beliefs, which for all intents and purposes functioned as "truths" for our author and his culture, were then legitimated by presenting the creator deity creating the world *as the author*

14. This is a shared cosmological perspective that is evidenced across the ancient world. The Greek god Poseidon, for example, gets his epithet "the earth-shaker" precisely because ancient man rationalized that earthquakes were caused by the violent shifting of the waters that the earth rested upon.

himself perceived it to be! In the end, what the god of Genesis 1:1–10 creates miraculously conforms to ancient Near Eastern man's perceptions and beliefs about the world, and not what we today know the world, and the larger cosmos, to be.

Thus any Creationist professing belief in the creation account of Genesis 1 is just being negligent about what this text actual says and does not say, as well as being disingenuous toward the text and the beliefs of its author. This again exemplifies the problem at hand as well as our modern educational malaise concerning the literature of the Bible. No so-called Creationist believes the creation account in Genesis 1, but rather feigns belief out of ignorance about the text and the beliefs, messages, and worldview expressed therein. Why? Because in truth these so-called Creationists are not interested in the beliefs and views of these ancient authors and the texts they wrote. If they were they would educate themselves about these texts, their authors, the historical circumstances that produced them, their historical and literary contexts, audiences, etc. Instead, they are more interested in and concerned about *their own beliefs* and how they can manipulate what has come to be deemed an authoritative text for our culture to legitimate their own views, beliefs, and agendas. I find this whole interpretive enterprise intellectually *and* spiritually damaging and dishonest, not to mention negligent of these ancient texts themselves and the beliefs and messages of their authors. Again our goal as mature, responsible readers should be to understand these ancient texts and their authors on *their terms* and in their historical and literary contexts, and to be able to faithfully reproduce *their beliefs*—not impose modern beliefs onto their literary compositions in some vain attempt to legitimate modern theological agendas. I will say more about this in the conclusion to this study.

Genesis 1:14–19—Yahweh's Eternal Festivals and the Creation of the Luminaries

The domed expanse or *raqi'a* that was made in vv. 6–8 to separate and hold back the waters above is now populated with the luminaries: sun, moon, and the stars—with no awareness of the individual distances of each luminary from the earth nor their actual size and place in the solar system. Here they are presented as three-dimensional buttons embedded within or upon this solid domed expanse, above which were the primordial waters above.

> Let there be lights in the domed expanse of the skies to separate
> between the day and the night, and let them be for signs, and for
> fixed times, and for days, and for years. (Gen 1:14)

Unlike modern man, ancient man constructed their calendars and measured the progression of time according to the celestial luminaries, predominantly the moon. The author of Genesis' first creation account depicts this idea by having the creator deity specify that these luminaries were created for this specific purpose. Yet the most fascinating and certainly the most revealing element here in v. 14 is the claim that these luminaries function, in part, as celestial markers for mankind to identify specific "fixed times." The Hebrew *mo'adim* is often translated as "seasons." But this translation does not capture the full semantic range implied in the word *mo'adim* and completely misses, I would argue, this author's subtle argument here.

A *mo'ed*, the singular form, was not only a fixed or appointed time (i.e., a specific day set by the appearance or position of the moon), but it was equally a fixed meeting, congregation, or more significantly festival. So the author of this text is claiming that the god who created the habitable world also embedded into the very fabric of the sky luminaries for observing the festival dates, the *mo'adim*, which mankind in general, but the Israelites specifically, were obliged to keep. Thus the luminaries were created in part so that mankind would know, observe, and keep Yahweh's festivals, these *mo'adim*.

What exactly are these "festival dates"? And why was this author interested in alluding to them in his creation account?

Out of the one hundred and sixty times that the word *mo'ed* appears in the Pentateuch, only eleven of them are from texts not written by the same priestly author who penned Genesis 1 (ch. 2). This is no coincidence. The Aaronid priestly guild responsible for the composition of this once independent scroll, which scholars conveniently label the Priestly source, was inflexible about the observance of the cult and Yahweh's *mo'adim*. In fact, according to this priestly guild, and thus also the god of its text, the observance of the sacrificial cult, Yahweh's festivals, and especially the Sabbath were all intimately woven into the very fabric of creation itself (ch. 3).

These *mo'adim*, "fixed times" or "festivals," alluded to in Genesis 1:14 are specifically identified in Leviticus 23, a text penned by the very same author who wrote Genesis 1:1—2:3 (this goes for all of Leviticus)—our Aaronid priest.

And Yahweh spoke to Moses saying, "Speak to the children of Israel and say to them concerning Yahweh's fixed times/festivals (*moʿadim*) which you shall call holy assemblies: 'These are my fixed times/festivals (*moʿadim*).'" (Lev 23:1–2)

The chapter then continues by listing Yahweh's "fixed times," which were all conceived of as holy days to be observed eternally. These fixed times are fixed by the position of the moon:

- On the 14th day of the 1st new moon is Yahweh's Passover—an "eternal law" according to this author and his Yahweh.

- On the 15th day of the 1st new moon is Yahweh's Festival of Unleavened Bread—also an "eternal law."

- On the day of the first harvest (this fixed time is not set by the moon) and 7 sabbatical weeks later on the 50th day is the Festival of Weeks, also proclaimed an "eternal law."

- On the 1st day of the 7th new moon is the Horn Blast Holy Day.

- On the 10th day of the 7th new moon is the Day of Atonement/Purgation, also an "eternal law."

- On the 15th day of the 7th new moon is the Festival of Booths, an "eternal law."

These, then, are the "fixed times" (*moʿadim*) to which Genesis 1:14 alludes. They refer to Yahweh's festivals which were to be observed eternally on penalty of being excommunicated.

What this author has subtly done is to argue that there is no excuse for the nonobservance of these *moʿadim*, of Yahweh's festivals, given that the creator god himself created the luminaries so that mankind would know when these fixed times/festivals occurred and thus be able to observe them. In other words, according to the views and beliefs of the priest(s) who wrote Genesis 1:1—2:3, the inviolable obligation for all Israelites to observe Yahweh's appointed holy days and festivals was directly woven into the very fabric of creation itself and indicated to mankind by way of the celestial luminaries which served as signs informing mankind when Yahweh's fixed festivals were to be celebrated. There is no excuse for noncompliance. According to this author, and the god of his text, both the Torah (the book of Leviticus) and the world as the creator God created it bear witness to the eternal obligation of mankind to observe and keep Yahweh's festivals.

This was the priestly writer's argument. Later readers who perceive and live in a different worldview cannot simply interpret away this author's beliefs, these "eternal laws" which were envisioned by the author of Genesis 1 as embedded into the very fabric of creation itself (ch. 3). Nor should they be allowed to claim hypocritically that they believe in this text and its author's beliefs when clearly they do not. This is to neglect and discard *this writer's* (and his god's) theological convictions and worldview. This is what I mean when I advocate that our goal as modern readers is to be honest to these ancient texts and to understand them *on their own terms and beliefs*, and be able to faithfully reproduce *their* beliefs and worldview—not how later readers repackaged them. From there the real conversation begins: "Hmm . . . This is a fascinating worldview. We certainly don't hold to it today, nor do we worship a god who does. Hmm again . . . Doesn't this mean that these 'eternal laws' were subjectively held 'truths' by this elite priestly guild, shaped by its cultural perspectives and worldview, and then transferred onto the god of its text? Hmm . . . What are the ramifications of this properly contextualized understanding of these ancient texts and what does it mean with respect to how we as a culture view the Bible today?"

Modern day Creationists, Fundamentalists, and literal Evangelicals who claim that they believe in the creation narrative of Genesis 1 are just being disingenuous toward this ancient text and the beliefs it expresses. The text does not validate nor support their claims. For the truth of the matter is that they do not in fact believe in the beliefs expressed in this text. A proper and correctly contextualized reading of the text itself convincingly demonstrates this point. Moreover, as we have seen with respect to the worldview expressed in Genesis 1:1–10, so too here: it is constructed on culturally shaped beliefs and perceptions about the world which were then transferred to the god of this text.

This can be illustrated here in another way. The fact that the moon is presented as "the lesser light" (1:16) when compared to the sun, "the greater light," reflects subjective and culturally held perceptions and beliefs endemic to the ancient world. Since the sun's light reflects off of the moon—a knowledge that our ancient biblical scribe did not possess—the moon was falsely perceived as producing its own light. This culturally conditioned "truth" was then transferred to the god of the priestly writer's text so that our biblical scribe presents God's creation of the moon as the creation of a light producing source, as he himself understood it! God now creates, not the moon *per se*, but *how the moon was perceived by our biblical author and his culture.* In other words, ancient texts do in fact represent the beliefs and perceptions of ancient peoples.

Genesis 1:20–28—Mankind, More than Just an Animal

Man is unlike any other animal of the earth. This truth was acknowledged and reflected upon by nearly every ancient culture. The Greek philosopher Plato proposed that man was divided between a lower animal part and an upper divine part, the immortal soul. He reasoned that man's divine intellect and soul set him apart from the rest of the animals. Ancient Egyptians also accorded man with an immortal soul, which originated from the gods and returned to them upon death of the physical body. And creation myths from ancient Egypt and Mesopotamia alike speak of the creation of man as part clay of the earth on the one hand, and part divine intelligence, divine blood, or divine breath on the other hand. Additionally, many of these same texts describe man as "the image of his creator god," and kings and Pharaohs throughout the Levant, including those from Israel, were imagined to be the sons of their respective cultural deity. It is therefore not surprising that this fundamental "truth" about the nature of man, that he was somehow different from the animals and that a part of him at some essential level originated from the divine, was also to be expressed in Genesis 1.

This is in fact the message behind our author's portrait of God's creation of mankind "in his image." But before we take a look at this, the creation of mankind must be seen in the framework our author intended his readers to see it—vis-à-vis the creation of the animals.

> And God said, "Let the waters swarm with a swarm of living beings (*nephesh hayah*), and let fowl fly above the earth (*'erets*) in front of the domed expanse (*raqi'a*) of the skies." And God created (*bara'*) the great sea-serpents and all living beings (*nephesh hayah*) that swim with which the waters swarm by their kind, and every winged fowl by its kind. (Gen 1:20–21)

> And God said: "Let the earth bring forth living beings (*nephesh hayah*) by their kind—beasts and reptiles—animals (*hayat*) of the earth by their kind." And it was so. And God made (*'asah*) the animals of the earth by their kind—the beasts by their kind and every reptile of the ground by its kind. (Gen 1:24–25)

The Hebrew *nephesh* denotes the life force that animates a living being or life in abstract terms—anything that has the breath of life in it: animals, humans, creatures. The adjective *hayah* basically means the same thing—living, alive. Thus "living beings" seems to best capture the intended sense here. This same phrase *nephesh hayah* also appears in the Yahwist creation account where, I will argue later, its use is significantly different from how it is used by the author of Genesis 1, and furthermore, when used to refer to both man (Gen 2:7) and the animals (Gen 2:19) violently contradicts the message of Genesis 1:24–27.

We must also strongly avoid and discourage the translation of *nephesh* by "soul." The word "soul" especially conceived of as "immortal soul" is a concept of Greek philosophy and is unknown to the Hebrew Bible and its authors. The concept doesn't emerge in Judaism until after Alexander the Great conquers the world at the end of the fourth century BCE, bringing with him Greek philosophical ideas into Judaism, and eventually into early Christianity. One clearly sees from its use in Genesis 1:20, 21, 24, and 30 that *nephesh* means life force, or that which has the breath of life in it, since "soul" is usually not a concept applied to fish, eels, worms, cattle, turkeys, bats, etc.

The point I wish to stress, no matter how one translates the expression *nephesh hayah*, is that it is never used in the creation of mankind, male and female, in Genesis 1:26–27. I am not saying that our author did not see mankind as a "living being"; of course he did. But I would argue that he consciously avoids using the expression in Genesis 1:26–27 because he is attempting to stress mankind's utter difference from the *nephesh hayah* or the *hayat* (animals) of the earth.

> And God said, "Let us make (*'asah*) mankind (*'adam*) in our image and after our likeness, and let them rule over the fish of the sea and over the fowl of the skies and over the beasts and over all the earth and over every reptile that crawls upon the earth." And God created (*bara'*) mankind in his image; in the image of God he created (*bara'*) it; male and female he created (*bara'*) them. (Gen 1:26–27)

There are two important differences our author emphasizes in his presentation of God's creation of the animals and of mankind, male and female.

First, the text stresses the inherent connection between the animals and the earth. This is emphasized by drawing our attention to God's imperative that the earth should "bring forth" living creatures (*nephesh hayah*), and that the earth's animals are somehow essentially connected to the earth. Then we are informed that the creator deity makes (*'asah*) the animals of the earth (*hayat ha'arets*)—beasts and reptiles—by their kind. Mankind, in contrast, is not of the earth. The focal point in the narrative changes at this point.

From the perspective of the author of Genesis 1, and contradictory to the views of Genesis 2 (below), mankind is not to be envisioned as equal to or on a par with the animals of the earth. The earth does not "bring forth" mankind in this creation myth—again in contrast to the second creation account. Furthermore, and again contradictory to Genesis 2:18, the animals are not seen as man's assistant helper (*'ezer*) or counterpart (*neged*), but rather mankind is to rule over them. He is of a different essence than they—not so according to Genesis 2, as we shall momentarily see. In fact, I might be tempted to argue that according to the author of Genesis 1, mankind is not to be conceived of as an animal of the earth! This brings me to my second point.

The repeated refrain "by its kind" as a descriptive for the manner in which the fowl of the skies, the fish of the seas, and the animals of the earth are created or made is not only a rhetorical device. It serves a thematic purpose as well whose function is to highlight mankind's utter difference to the animals, only this time with respect to the manner of how he/she is created. It is difficult to say what exactly our author intended by the expression "by its kind." It would seem that the idea conveyed is that each life form was distinct, that a cow for example, or what a cow is, is distinctly defined "by its own kind." At any event, the expression is used to convey how radically different this creation "by its kind" is to the creation of mankind. For unlike the living beings of the earth (*hayat ha'arets*), mankind is not created according to its own kind but rather in the image of the divine beings: "in our image and after our likeness." That is to say, according to the author of this creation account, God made every living being of the earth—except that of mankind—according to its own kind. Mankind, however, was not created after its own kind, but rather in the image and likeness of God.

The ideas expressed by our author here are again not some divinely ordained and objective description of the origins of mankind. Rather, like everything else in this creation account, they are the expression of the views and beliefs of our author and his culture. It is *our author* who perceives mankind as radically different from the animals that populate the earth. And this difference causes him to compose a creation narrative wherein these differences are expressed. Unlike the living beings of the earth, each made according to their own kind, mankind, on the contrary, is created in the image and likeness of the divine beings! That seems to be our author's message.

By way of concluding this section, I might encourage my readers to start thinking about how this later sixth-century BCE creation myth functioned in relationship to the earlier Yahwist account now preserved in Genesis 2:4b—3:24, which we will shortly look at. Following the work of my colleagues,[15] it has been hypothesized that the Priestly writer was writing a creation narrative to replace or subvert the earlier eight-century BCE Yahwist creation account, but due to an unforeseen later editorial endeavor both accounts were preserved side-by-side. At any event, the point to mull over, to which we will return later, is that we can see the Priestly writer's concerns here. For in the earlier Yahwist text, man, that is, the sole creation of Adam, is in no way distinguished from the animals of the earth. Even after he receives Yahweh's breath, Adam is still made of the same essential material that the animals are made of, the 'adamah (the ground), and only still merely becomes what the animals themselves are referred to as—a nephesh hayah (Gen 2:7, 19). I would propose that this is just one of the specific concerns and disagreements that the Priestly writer had with this older tradition that he himself inherited. So what did he do? He rewrote it in accord with his own views and beliefs on the matter—rewriting mankind above and distinct from the animals of the earth, not equivalent to them!

Genesis 2:2–3—The Sabbath: Sacred Time Embedded in the Creation

> And on the seventh day God finished his work which he had made; and he rested (*shabat*) on the seventh day from all his work which he had made. And God blessed the seventh day and made it holy, because on it he rested from all his work which God created and had made. (Gen 2:2–3)

On the seventh and last day of this creation account, our author not only presents the deity resting from his creative work, but more significantly consecrating and blessing the seventh day as holy. That is to say, the creator god creates and proclaims the last day of creation as a holy day of rest, a Sabbath—distinct from the previous six nonsacred or common days.

This is a significant point which is largely neglected, misunderstood, and/or interpreted away by our so-called modern day Creationists and

---

15. See especially Carr, *Reading the Fractures of Genesis*.

biblical literalists in general who, despite their claims, do not actually believe in the creation of the world as presented here in Genesis 1:1—2:3. For they, as do all of us, perceive and live in a world which is radically at odds to that envisioned in this text and believed by its author, and by extension *his* god! We do not believe nor perceive the world to be inherently, essentially, or categorically divided up into sacred dates set by the lunar calendar, and a weekly recurring sacred day, which was created as sacred and holy by the creator God himself when he created the earth and the skies. This is what our author believed (ch. 3). This was his worldview. This was his creationism. It is not, in other words, the creationism touted by modern day Creationists! More will be said about this in chapter 3.

As we saw with the creation of the luminaries for the purpose of being able to observe and thus keep Yahweh's holy festivals, the same applies here: the Sabbath is to be observed precisely because the God of creation created the seventh day as a holy, sacred day when he created the world. This is our author's message. And it explains why the punishment for nonobservance was so severe. From the perspective of our author and his priestly guild, to blatantly neglect and not keep that which the creator God created at creation as a sacred, distinct, holy day was blasphemous pure and simply. The punishment? Swift and inviolable death.[16]

Thus according to the elite priestly guild that penned Genesis 1:1—2:3, the God of creation not only created the things of the visible world as it was perceived through the cultural lens of our ancient Israelite scribe, but he additionally created specific lunar dates and intervals of time as sacred and these holy days were embedded into his creation. That the seventh day was created and proclaimed as a consecrated holy day to be distinguished and observed on a weekly basis from the previous six nonsacred or common days was as much of an uncompromising fact inherent in the created world for our author as the skies or the sun above. Any violation of this created order, that is, what God himself created, was met with a swift death. One cannot neglect or breach an inherent, god-created law of the created world. That is what the priestly writer was getting at. Doing profane or common work on the Sabbath not only blasphemed the very day that the creator god created in its essence and nature as holy, but it also blasphemed the whole of creation, as well as the creator God himself who deemed and declared the seventh day holy to himself and to his people—a blasphemous act, it

---

16. See Exod 31:12–17; 35:1–2; Num 15:32–36—all from the pen of the same author. Discussed in ch. 3.

must be acknowledged, repeated today on a weekly bases by any individual claiming that he/she believes in this text! For an honest and objective reading of the text itself reveals the ugly truth of the matter: that Creationists do not believe in this text, the world depicted in it, and the beliefs associated with this ancient priestly worldview. Rather they interpret away this author's beliefs and worldview under the pretext of later theological lenses and beliefs while nevertheless imposing their own beliefs and worldview onto this text and then claiming belief in the text!

Chapter 3 is devoted to looking more specifically at Yahweh's holy days, including the Sabbath, which according to the priestly guild responsible for writing this text were embedded into the very fabric of the created world itself by the creator deity at creation.

What the Author—and the God—of Genesis 1:1—2:3 Believed according to the Text

Since many Creationists, Fundamentalists, and Jews and Christians of various persuasions claim that they believe in the Bible, or specifically in our case, believe in the creation narrative of Genesis 1:1—2:3, I've decided to list this author's—and by extension his god's—beliefs in a clear and orderly fashion as a sort of summation to our culturally contextualized reading of his text.

As has been repeatedly voiced throughout this chapter, our aim here is to reproduce as faithfully and objectively as possible the beliefs of the author of Genesis 1:1—2:3 as evidenced by an understanding and reading of his text on its own terms and as a product of its own historical and literary world. The author that penned the creation account now found at Genesis 1:1—2:3 had a very unique priestly vision of the world and a set of beliefs that, in large part, were shaped by and shared throughout the larger ancient Near Eastern world within which he lived. And these beliefs themselves were most likely formed as the result of what ancient peoples saw and perceived about their world and the conclusions they naturally drew from these limited empirical observations. Therefore, Genesis 1 is an account of the nature of the world and its origins *as its author perceived it*. Moreover, his culturally conditioned perceptions and beliefs about the world and its origin were then projected onto the god of his composition so that, in turn, it is God who then creates the world that he himself, our author, perceived and experienced. These then were his beliefs and by extension those of the creator God of his text:

1. That God created the earth (dry, habitable land, not the planet) and the skies out of preexistent, undefined, and uninhabitable "earth" that was immersed in a deep, dark watery abyss.

2. That creation was an act of separating this primordial matter (earth and water) out, subduing it, and forming it into a habitable, life-sustaining world.

3. That the source of day's light is an inherent and essential property of day itself; its source is not the sun.

4. That God created day as light itself or daylight.

5. That night is the original primordial darkness.

6. That God subdued the primordial untamed waters by creating a solid domed expanse in the midst of these waters, thereby separating them, now above and below this barrier.

7. That the sky *is* this solid crystalline domed barrier.

8. That the sky's function, as God created it, is to keep back the waters above it.

9. That the sky is blue because of the waters above it.

10. That the sky, this solid domed expanse holding back the waters above, touched the waters below at the horizons.

11. That God subdued the waters below, which were half of the preexistent primordial waters, and caused them to gather together, thereby creating seas.

12. That earth, specifically dry, habitable, life-supporting land—not the planet—emerged from the depths of these now tamed seas, previously the untamed primordial waters.

13. That this earth "floated" upon or was supported by the waters below.

14. That earth itself brought forth plants and vegetation, each by its own kind.

15. That God created and placed the sun, moon, and all the stars together in or upon the solid domed expanse that he had made earlier, above which were the waters above.

16. That these luminaries were created to regulate and to distinguish between the day and the night, not to create day (daylight) and night.

17. That these luminaries moved through or upon this domed barrier.

18. That the moon produces its own light.

19. That God created the luminaries, in part, to indicate when the months began, and on what days Yahweh's festivals (Sabbath, Passover, Unleavened Bread, Horn-Blast Holy Day, Day of Atonement, and Booths) fell and were to be observed (ch. 3).

20. That the observance of these festivals or holy days were eternal laws whose nonobservance was punishable by death or excommunication (ch. 3).

21. That God created the luminaries, particularly the moon, to serve as a calendar system, each new moon beginning a new month.

22. That God created the living beings of the waters below, each by their kind.

23. That God created the birds, each by their kind.

24. That God created the animals of the earth, each by their kind.

25. That in opposition to the creation of the animals according to their kinds, God created mankind, male and female together, after his own image.

26. That there existed a plurality of divine beings or a divine council of some sort.

27. That God created all of this in six days.

28. That God created and consecrated the seventh day as a sacred, holy day set apart from the previous six common days.

29. That God rested from his work on the seventh day and therefore man too must rest from his work on the seventh day.

30. That the seventh-day Sabbath observance is reckoned on the seventh day from the new moon's appearance and each seventh consecutive day thereafter until the next new moon when the counting starts anew.

31. That anyone caught doing work on the seventh day from the new moon (that is, not observing the Sabbath) blasphemes the creator God *and* his creation and is therefore to be stoned to death by commandment from the creator God himself (ch. 3).

32. That the Sabbath was an eternal law and eternal covenant to be observed forever on penalty of death.

These, then, are the expressed beliefs of the author of Genesis
1:1—2:3—in fact, just a small fraction of what he believed and perceived
as "truth" according to his perception of the world and his priestly ideology (see ch. 2). We furthermore observe that one of the literary techniques
employed by this ancient scribe was to place his beliefs, perception of the
world, and even ideology on the lips of his god, in this case Yahweh. This
literary convention becomes even more visible when we read the rest of
the text that this author originally penned (ch. 2) comparatively with other
texts of the Pentateuch, most notably Deuteronomy, whose author also uses
the same literary technique to legitimate radically different and at times
contradictory beliefs and laws.[17]

So what percentage of the beliefs above, which represent the world
as seen by an elite guild of ancient Israelite priests, are seriously believed
by our so-called modern day Creationists? I would venture to say an extremely small percentage. Again, the particular point is not whether we
of the modern world share *some of* the beliefs found in this ancient text.
For we could find tenets and proverbial snippets from a variety of different
texts from the ancient world that might still speak to us today. Rather the
goal, as I have been stressing, is to be able to acknowledge the beliefs of
the author of this ancient text and faithfully reproduce his worldview and
belief system. Then, if we felt inclined, we could compare his worldview and
belief system with ours. But by no means should we employ an interpretive
methodology that *interprets away* this author's—and his god's—beliefs, or
one that imposes our beliefs and scientific perception of the world onto
his worldview in an attempt to legitimate our own beliefs about the world.
Again, understanding this ancient text *as its author intended* requires that
we allow the text to invite us into its worldview and belief system—not
impose ours onto it or interpret his (and his god's) away under the pretext
of later interpretive frameworks and theological constructs.

Certainly one may still believe, for example, that God, however envisioned, created the world or created mankind. But like the beliefs expressed
in Genesis 1:1—2:3 these also are subjective, culturally defined beliefs. We
saw, for example, that the author of Genesis 1's beliefs and perceptions about
the nature and origin of *his* world were culturally conditioned and part of

17. Treated fully in my forthcoming *Understanding Bible Contradictions*.

his own subjective experience and perception of his world. Similarly, so too were his ideas about the nature and origin of mankind. These beliefs were also shaped by the limited empirical knowledge and cultural perceptions about the world as shared throughout the ancient civilizations of the Near East. Furthermore, pontificating on one shared belief out of approximately thirty others which this ancient priest also firmly believed in is not even remotely close to *believing in* this ancient text and its worldview. In fact, the most significant belief expressed by this author in his creation narrative is the observance of the Sabbath. No one in today's society, especially Creationists, believe that God the creator created and designated a specific sacred day—an "eternal law" in the words of our author—into the very fabric of the created world, which was to be calculated by counting every seventh day from the new moon, and whose sacredness was to be observed and kept on penalty of death! We simply do not perceive our world in the terms and categories that ancient priests did (see ch. 2). Indeed, our worldview and beliefs stand in stark opposition to the beliefs and worldview presented in Genesis 1:1—2:3. Our world, or the objective, scientifically verifiable world, is not the world created in Genesis 1:1—2:3. This is what the text tells us when read on its own terms. So anyone claiming otherwise is just being disingenuous to the beliefs of this author and negligent of the very text that he himself composed and what it actually claims and does not claim about the nature and origins of the world and of man and woman.

In the end, then, ancient texts do in fact represent the views and beliefs of ancient peoples and cultures. I really shouldn't have to argue for this. And learning about the literary conventions employed by the ancient scribes who wrote these texts, we also come to realize that their unique beliefs and worldviews were legitimated and presented as the beliefs and worldview of that particular culture's deity. We see this throughout the literature of the ancient Near East, but especially in the biblical canon since it is in fact a collection of ancient texts spanning almost a thousand years. Even a close comparison of Genesis 1 and 2 reveals competing and contradictory mindsets and perceptions about the nature and origins of the world and of man and woman. And the differing beliefs and worldview that underlie the second creation myth were also presented and legitimated by placing them on Yahweh's lips.

GENESIS 2:4B–24 ON ITS OWN TERMS AND IN ITS OWN HISTORICAL AND LITERARY CONTEXT

From the opening verse of the second creation account, or if my reader prefers right at Genesis 2:4b, we notice stark differences in the text's tone, style, vocabulary, message, presentation, perspective, and thematic and theological emphases. These will be brought out in the forthcoming textual analysis. These differences should not be ignored or disingenuously interpreted away by imposing an exterior theological framework created centuries after these texts were written and by a readership that knew nothing about the authors of these texts, when they were written, why, and for whom. Rather these textual differences should be seen as a product of the text's historical and literary context, and even embraced for what they are—the mark of a different scribal hand, a different textual tradition, a variant version of the same story.

Stories were as much a part of the ancient world as the television is for us today. People told and heard stories on a daily basis. It was part of their lifeblood. Stories defined a people's identity, explained the origins of current political and religious institutions, and preserved traditional beliefs, worldviews, and customs.

Many stories in the ancient world enjoyed a long oral tradition before they were finally written down, and many of these same stories have their origins in older stories that were borrowed and modified from other or earlier peoples. For instance, many of the stories now preserved in Genesis and Exodus are modified versions of stories that existed in the cultures and traditions of Israel's older contemporaries. Stories about the creation of the world, a cataclysmic universal flood, digging wells as land markers, the naming of important cultic sites, gods giving laws to their people, gods decreeing that their people build them temples and sanctuaries, and even stories about gods decreeing the possession of land to their people were all part of the cultural and literary matrix of the ancient Near East. In many cases alternate versions of these stories existed. A people living at one place and time might tell the story that they inherited from their forefathers or an earlier indigenous culture differently in order to suit the needs of their community, or to better represent its changing views and beliefs.

The ancient Israelites were no exception. They told stories, retold stories, modified their stories, recited them at festivals, and eventually wrote them down, collected them, and codified them as scripture. The Bible as it has come down to us preserves numerous stories, and many of them are duplicates—that is, a traditional story that was told in one manner at one place and time, and told in a variant manner at another place and time. In the end, these different versions were written down by scribes and thenceforth became unalterable. Later, editors who collected Israel's various stories preserved both versions of the story, even when they contradicted one another, or a later story was written to replace an earlier version. In fact, doublets—two versions of the same story—have always served as good indicators for identifying the Bible's different textual traditions or sources. Nearly all of the contradictory stories and even competing "histories" found in the Bible were created because of an editorial decision made by later scribes who deemed it important to preserve variant versions of ancient Israel's stories.[18]

The two creation stories that open the book of Genesis are exactly that—variations on the same story. And these two versions of the creation story were written by two different scribes or guilds, to address different historical and/or religious concerns and perspectives, for two distinct historical audiences, and most likely influenced by two different versions of the creation story as it had already been told throughout the ancient Near East! We have already seen how the author of Genesis 1:1—2:3 borrowed themes and perspectives shared throughout the cultures of the ancient Near Eastern world, and modified them to suit his own beliefs and agenda. This is the same case for Genesis' second creation account. It too was influenced by ancient Near Eastern literary genres that existed prior to its composition. Textually we see that the story that starts at Genesis 2:4b proceeds as if the first creation account never occurred. This story never acknowledges, alludes to, shares, or builds upon any of the narrative, thematic, stylistic, or theological elements found in the creation account in Genesis 1:1—2:3. To the contrary, as we will see, this second creation account actually negates many of the themes and claims found in the first creation account, and frankly this is because it was written separately, by a different scribe, and centuries before the creation account now occupying Genesis 1:1—2:3 was written. Despite these two stories' thematic and stylistic differences, they were preserved on a single scroll by scribes living centuries after they were written *precisely because* they represented variant sacred traditions.

Of course, readers of the Bible did not always possess this knowledge, even though the differences in Genesis' two creation accounts had long

---

18. These contradictory stories and competing "histories" are the topic of my forthcoming *Understanding Bible Contradictions*.

been noted from antiquity to the modern era. It wasn't until the beginning of the nineteenth century that we realized that these differences were the result of an editorial endeavor initiated by scribes living in the fifth century BCE who sought to preserve the various textual traditions of ancient Israel by combining them together on a single scroll. But these discoveries rest on even earlier ones, representing a cumulative academic endeavor that had its origins in the Enlightenment. Said differently, knowledge about the composite nature of the biblical text was all but unknown to readers of the Bible until the emergence of biblical scholarship during the Enlightenment.

The emergence of the source hypothesis in the early eighteenth century, for instance, was initially prompted by the work of three scholars who each individually drew the same conclusion from the textual data that the book of Genesis reveals when studiously read. The German Lutheran minister Henning Bernhard Witter, the French physician for Louis XV, Jean Astruc, and a professor of Göttingen University by the name of Johann Gottfried Eichhorn each separately came to the conclusion that the Pentateuch is a composite of, at least, two once independent sources. It was Witter who in the early eighteenth century (1711) postulated a two-source hypothesis initially based on the distinction of two different appellations for Israel's god in the opening creation accounts of the book of Genesis, 'elohim and Yahweh. However, it wasn't until the 1753 study by Astruc[19] that the impact of this discovery was felt. Astruc not only labeled these two sources the Elohistic (from the Hebrew 'elohim) and the Jehovistic (from the mistaken medieval pronunciation of the tetragrammaton, YHWH), but he also noticed that these two sources exhibited other differences besides the two distinct appellations of Israel's deity, and furthermore that these differences extended throughout the entire book of Genesis. Most impressively, this two-source hypothesis was able to explain successfully the book of Genesis' duplicate narratives, discordant chronologies, narrative inconsistencies, differing portraits of Israel's god, and its numerous contradictions! All of these were the result of a centuries-later editorial endeavor that brought together two once separate ancient traditions or versions of the same stories.

Today, although much has changed in our understanding of the Bible's composite nature since the eighteenth century, the view that the Pentateuch is composed of different and competing textual traditions, which has been

---

19. *Conjectures sur les mémoires originauz dont il paroit que Moyse s'est servi pour composer le livre de la Génèse* [*Conjectures on the original sources which Moses apparently used in composing the book of Genesis*].

continuously tested, verified, and reconfirmed over the past hundred years, is accepted by all serious biblical scholars. Although scholars may debate about the dates of composition of these sources, who specifically wrote them and to whom, and why they were redacted together and under what form, all critics agree that the Bible as we now possess it is a composite literary work, formed over a thousand-year period and representing the views and beliefs of diverse scribes, priests, and theologians living in drastically different historical circumstances and influenced by ever-changing religious and political needs, agendas, and convictions. The placement of this second creation account immediately after the first one is just one example of where and how these conflating traditions were preserved and brought together. There are literally hundreds of other places in the Bible where two or more once separate and variant textual traditions were stitched together—leaving behind duplicate stories, narrative inconsistencies, contradictions, and competing ideologies, theologies, and even law codes.[20] Here we are interested in only the first two creation accounts.

Genesis 2:4b—Observing Thematic and Stylistic Differences

There are several differences that are immediately noticeable in the opening verse (Gen 2:4b) of this second creation account. A literal translation runs: "In the day that god Yahweh made earth and skies . . ."

We immediately notice that the creator deity is now specified by name, Yahweh.[21] This feature is unique to both this creation account and the textual tradition to which it belongs, unceremoniously named the Yahwist. This source (J) earns its name because its author consistently uses the name of Israel's deity, Yahweh, throughout his composition. Even though the divine name appears approximately 1,800 times in the Pentateuch alone, the other Pentateuchal sources (Elohist, Deuteronomist, and Priestly) refrain from using the name Yahweh prior to its revelation to Moses in Exodus. Only the Yahwist text, in other words, affirms and acknowledges contrary to the other sources that the name Yahweh was known to, and frequently invoked by, the patriarchs prior to its revelation. It is for this reason that the Yahwist tradition does not narrate a revelation of the divine name.

20. For a detailed treatment of these variant traditions and how they interact with one another, see my forthcoming *Understanding Bible Contradictions*.

21. See n1.

According to this tradition, it was known right from the first generation of mortals (Gen 4:26).

As previously discussed, the specific use of the name of the god of Israel throughout this textual tradition is really the least significant of the differences between the first creation account's portrait of God and that of the second account. More dramatic is the stark anthropomorphism that this scribe uses to portray Yahweh. In Genesis 2:4b—3:24 Yahweh is depicted *forming* man from the dust of the earth, *breathing* into the man's nostrils, *planting* a garden, *placing* the man in the garden, *forming* animals from the ground, *building* a woman from the man's rib, *walking* in the garden, *speaking* to his creation, and finally *making* garments of skins for the human pair. This type of anthropomorphism, that is, presenting a deity in human terms, is only found in the Yahwist tradition and for the most part attests to its antiquity.

But this textual tradition's anthropomorphism goes even further than this. Yahweh is often depicted talking to himself, repenting, grieving, and raging with anger on numerable incidences. He talks face-to-face with the patriarchs, walks side-by-side with them, and even eats with Abraham on one occasion. More surprisingly, this tradition displays no indication that this conception of the god was problematic. Certainly the anthropomorphism of the Yahwist tradition becomes problematic for later scribes, who either disagreed with this author's portrait of Israel's god or understood the godhead on a higher theological plane. The later Deuteronomist, for example, puts forth a conception of Yahweh that is without form; no image can be formed of him, and he only communicates to mortals as a formless voice from the heavens. Likewise, it has been argued that one of the reasons that the later Priestly tradition rewrote the Yahwist creation story was to rectify or replace the anthropomorphic depiction of Yahweh in this older account with a more majestic, impersonal, and certainly less anthropomorphic portrait of Israel's god. The Priestly source rarely if ever presents Yahweh in the anthropomorphic manner adopted by the earlier Yahwist scribe.

Another immediately observable point of conflict between the opening statement of this second creation account and Genesis 1:1—2:3 is the time referent "in the day." For in the first creation account, God does not create the earth and the skies on the same day. In fact, the first creation account tells us that the skies, the domed expanse or *raqi'a*, was created on the second day, and earth, that is, dry land, emerged from the waters below on the third day. Furthermore, contrary to the claims of Genesis 2:4b—7, man was not created on any of the days on which the earth and the skies were created. According to the first creation account, the days on which God created the earth (day 3) and the skies (day 2) come and go without the creation of man (day 6).

Additionally, it would be incorrect to regard the temporal referent "in the day" in Genesis 2:4b as a general abstract statement, particularly if one assumed, falsely, the same authorship for these two creation accounts. For not only does this time referent clash with the previous account's symmetry and chronology, but more significantly the temporal referent of Genesis 2:4b does not reflect the same precision and formulaic presentation of the chronology of creation so emphatically and carefully laid out throughout Genesis 1:1—2:3. This is because the same author did not write this verse!

In other words, the orderly, formulaic, and precise use of both language, themes, and the chronology of creation so ritualistically accentuated throughout the entirety of Genesis 1:1—2:3 is simply abandoned and negated—when erroneously assuming the same author—by the imprecise, incorrect, or even abstract temporal reference of v. 2:4b concerning which day(s) god Yahweh created "earth and skies." Again, this is because v. 2:4b, and the story that follows, was penned by a different scribe. Contrary to the fist creation account with its temporal precision, the second creation account merely commenced: "In the day that god Yahweh made earth and skies . . ."

Finally, according to this second creation account, earth, the skies, man, plants, animals, and lastly woman were all created on one day: "in the day that god Yahweh made earth and skies" he also formed man, then apparently plants, animals, and lastly woman. This radically contradicts with all of Genesis 1:1—2:3 on thematic, stylistic, and even theological grounds! The subsequent creation of each one of these life forms in the second creation account—man, plants, animals, and woman—is chronologically dissimilar and utterly contradictory to the presentation, order, and manner in which the creation of each one of these life forms is presented in the first creation account. In sum, these differences are not the mark of the same author, but rather a textual indicator that another whole creation narrative begins here, one that furthermore commences by claiming, contrary to the narrative of Genesis 1:1—2:3, that neither man, vegetation, nor animals have yet been created! Genesis 2:4b therefore sets the scene, both thematically and stylistically, for a second creation account, one which commenced: "In the day that god Yahweh made earth and skies . . ."

Besides differences in the treatment of thematic material, Genesis 2:4b also reveals the hand of a different author on stylistic and linguistic grounds. The verb choice of 2:4b evidences the mindset of a different author. In this verse, the author chooses the general verb "to make," in Hebrew *'asah*. Although we find the verb *'asah* also employed in the first creation account, and specifically in reference to the making of the domed expanse, the verb of choice for the author of the first creation account in expressing God's creative work is *bara'*, "to create." In fact this is the verb this author consciousiy chooses for his opening verse: "In the beginning when God created (*bara'*) the skies and the earth . . ."

Its meaning, moreover, is quite different from that of *'asah*, which simply means "to make." *Bara'* denotes a creative act which brings something into existence by means of separating or dividing it out. Thus in the first creation account, the creator deity creates (*bara'*) earth by separating it out from the waters below and converting it into dry habitable land, and the skies by separating the original primordial water mass into two. Thus, the use of the verb *'asah* in Genesis 2:4b not only marks a linguistic difference, but it also displays the mindset of a different author who conceived of creation in different terms from those employed by the author of the first creation account. Simply put, the author of Genesis 1:1 would not have used—I would argue consciously avoided using—*'asah* for his opening statement. It would have been an ill-conceived verb choice for this author.

Conversely, the author of Genesis 2:4b—3:24 never uses the verb *bara'* anywhere in his composition! This especially holds true for this author's presentation of the creation, or rather fabrication, of man. Again, this is not just a difference in verb choice, but a larger difference revealing how each one of our authors conceived and imagined the deity's creative act. More on this below.

Another stylistic difference noticeable in the Hebrew of v. 2:4b which also evidences the mark of a different scribal hand is the absence of the Hebrew particle *'eth* which is an untranslated particle used after a verb to mark a direct object in the accusative case. It is not translated in English since its purpose is just to indicate the direct object. Thus Genesis 1:1 in Hebrew is: *bara' 'elohim 'eth hashamayim we'eth ha'arets*—literally, "God created the skies and the earth." The two *'eth*'s are not translated; they serve merely to mark the direct object of the verb: "the skies" (*ha shamayim*) and "the earth" (*ha 'arets*). But Genesis 2:4b is quite different.

In the Hebrew of 2:4b not only is 'eth not employed, but neither is the definite article ha, "the." Here is the Hebrew of Genesis 2:4b: 'asot yahweh 'elohim 'erets weshamayim—literally, "God Yahweh made earth and skies." The conscious choice to avoid the use of 'eth in Genesis 2:4b and the article ha most likely reflects this author's desire to express a more poetic, even archaic, style: 'eth is rarely used in poetry. Conversely, the author who penned Genesis 1:1 does not, and would not have, written his Hebrew in this manner, that is, without using the direct object marker 'eth, and without the use of the definite article ha. There is also the added difference that the order is inverted between these two verses—"the skies and the earth" and "earth and skies"—which on its own might not mean anything, but together with the differences reviewed above is a further indication of another author's hand.

In sum, the Hebrew of Genesis 2:4b and in fact the Hebrew of all of the second creation account evidences a more poetic style and tone, and has a more storyteller feeling to it. The Hebrew of Genesis 1:1—2:3, on the other hand, evidences the hand of an educated pedantic scribe. It is no surprise then to learn that the first creation account was written by a sixth-century elite priestly guild at a time when Israel was a temple-state; while the second creation account was written by a secular scribe, a storyteller from the days of old. These different social groups are reflected in the style and tone of the Hebrew itself.

The textual data are overwhelming thus far and we've only looked at the first five words of Genesis 2:4b—3:24's story! The data convincingly demonstrate, and will further corroborate, that this creation account, a second account, was written by a different author whose Hebrew, vocabulary, portrait of Israel's deity, and conception and ideas about the creation of the world and of mankind were all vastly different from, and in many ways contrary to, those of the author who penned the first creation account. People who try to harmonize these differences away are just not being honest to the texts and their individual authors, and more severely have placed their own beliefs *about* the texts above the texts themselves, what they themselves say, and the views and beliefs of their independent authors. It's time we started being honest to these texts by acknowledging these authors' competing beliefs and messages.

Genesis 2:5—Man and Rain: Prerequisites to the Creation of Plants

The differences so far illustrated in just the opening verse of the second creation account (Gen 2:4b) become more pronounced as we move through the narrative. Genesis 2:5–7, for example, evidences a dramatic shift in emphasis, thematic material, message, vocabulary, and style.

By way of introduction it might be said that the perspective adopted in these opening verses and indeed throughout this entire creation narrative is an agricultural one, focusing on man's relationship to the ground and to the vegetation of that ground. Already in vv. 5–7 there is a heightened emphasis on plants as agricultural produce, their fields, the rain required for growing that produce, and man for cultivating or tilling these fields and its vegetation. Man, in other words, is essentially defined in relation to the ground whence he was made, and specifically in relation to tilling the ground to produce his livelihood (Gen 2:5, 15; 3:23). By contrast, woman is essentially defined in relation to man, whence she was made (more below).

The portrait of male and female—note the difference in vocabulary—created together in the image of the god(s) and thus distinct from the earth and the animals of the earth is not only absent in this second narrative but it was not even a conceivable idea to its author. His message and focus are radically different and lie elsewhere. As is my custom, I shall attempt to be as honest as possible *to his message and beliefs*—not those of later readers.

Thematically Genesis 2:5–6 not only brings us back to a point in the assembled narrative *prior to* the creation of plants, animals, and man—which in and of itself contradicts the creation narrative of Genesis 1:1—2:3 in its entirety—but its opening setting specifically negates Genesis 1:9–10, 11–12, 29–30, and for that matter the entire conclusion of the first creation account. Just look at these verses and observe what is being presented thematically and how this is being presented stylistically and linguistically.

> And God said: "*Let the earth bring forth* plants, *vegetation ('eseb) yielding seed, fruit trees producing fruit of its own kind whose seed is in it*, upon the earth." And it was so. And the *earth brought forth* plants, *vegetation yielding seed of its own kind*, and *trees producing fruit whose seed was in it of its own kind*. And God saw that it was good. (Gen 1:11–12 [P])

> And God said: "Behold! I have given you every *vegetation ('eseb) bearing seed* which is on the face of the whole earth and every *tree*

in which there is the fruit of a tree bearing seed. To you it will be for food." (Gen 1:29 [P])

In the day that god Yahweh made earth and skies, and all *shrub of the field* had not yet been in the earth and all *vegetation ('eseb) of the field* had not yet grown, for god Yahweh had not caused it to rain upon the earth and no man yet existed to till the ground . . . (Gen 2:4b–5 [J])

When read one after the other, the passages above not only evidence noticeable differences in narrative quality, tone, style, and vocabulary, but also in their thematic presentation of earth, the creation of plants and mankind, and most importantly the rationale behind that creation.

First, after having already created all of the earth's plants, "all vegetation yielding seed," and "all trees in which there is the fruit of a tree yielding seed"—note the language and style of this author—and decreeing them as food for all of mankind and the animals of the earth alike, the story that begins at Genesis 2:4b–5 proceeds as if none of these things have yet happened. In fact, the story and its author display no knowledge of the preceding narrative and of the fact that *all* of the earth's vegetation had already been brought into existence according to this account—frankly because this first creation account had not yet been written! Rather vv. 5–7, as with all of Genesis 2:4b—3:24, were written independently of Genesis 1:1—2:3, centuries earlier, and display the mark of a different style and linguistic register. In short, this is the beginning of a new and radically different creation story, one that is furthermore making contradictory claims about the earth and the creation of plants, man, the animals, and lastly woman.

Second, its focus is radically different as well. Unlike the first creation account, this story stresses a reason *why* god Yahweh has not yet created plants—because there is no water yet available, in the form of rain, to give the plants what they require in order for them to grow, and because man has not yet been created in order to till the ground so that the vegetation may produce food. These are revealing details and are completely absent in the first creation narrative. According to this narrative with its culturally conditioned agricultural perspective, Yahweh has not yet caused the earth to produce plants and vegetation (*contra* Gen 1:11–12, 29–30) *because* he has not yet created a means to water these plants and vegetation, nor the means through which their ground is to be tilled. What is implied in these opening verses is that Yahweh *cannot* create plants and vegetation yet because neither rain nor man have yet been created.

In other words, the author of this creation account is making a poignant agricultural statement: rain, or water in general, and man are needed for any vegetation to grow. Their existence serves as a prerequisite to the creation of plants. In this creation account's perspective, we must of necessity move immediately from the creation of earth and skies (2:4b) to the creation of man (2:7), because according to this author's worldview plants cannot be created prior to man. Thus similar to what we found in the first creation story, so too here: this author's culturally formed perspective of his world shaped how he told the story of creation.

Third, what is implied in all of this is that the earth or ground is in a very different state of existence than the earth created in Genesis 1:9–10. In this second account the earth is dry, barren, and initially lacking moisture (but see v. 6). In the previous account it is inherently moist and fecund emerging as it does from the waters below. From the perspective of the author who penned the first creation account, earth emerges from the waters below, is inherently fecund, and immediately generates on God's command plants, fruit-bearing trees, and all forms of seed-bearing vegetation. That's radically different from what we have here in this account. Furthermore, in the first creation account there is no creation of man between the earth's appearance (v. 9) and the generation of all its plants, trees, and vegetation each after its own kind (vv. 11–12). Man is simply not seen as the prerequisite to the creation of plants in this creation account; it was written to accommodate a different perspective and goal. Additionally, there is not a hint of interest in man's relationship to the ground and its tilling, and in fact the first creation account goes out of its way to present man's creation divorced from any relationship to the earth by presenting a portrait of him, and her, being created in God's image and likeness.

Thus, contrary to the elite priestly scribe who penned Genesis 1:1–2:3 under the influence of the literary traditions of Mesopotamia, which were themselves shaped by the empirical observations of their geographical reality—a fertile earth resting upon the delta regions—the perspective represented by the author who penned Genesis 2:4b–25 was born from the hard realities of the Canaanite landscape, where its dry, hard ground needed the rains to fertilize its produce. This is illustrated in v. 6 with the mention of a mist which comes up from the earth. In this account, earth doesn't emerge from the waters below as in the first creation account, but is presented as dry and barren at its creation and needing to be moistened by the rains above or the mist and springs which bubble up from the earth below, which indeed did populate the Canaanite landscape. So our perspective, that is, the author's subjective perspective and cultural biases, have radically changed, and these changes cause us to have a radically different depiction of the creation of earth, plants, and as we shall see, man and woman.

Stylistically, there are also a number of differences that clearly indicate the mark of a different scribe with a different writing style and emphasis. These differences highlight our author's interests and even cultural perspectives and beliefs, and are already evident in vv. 5–7. They may be categorized as: interest in etiologies, etymologies, wordplay and puns, a storyteller style of narration, more poetic sentence syntax and tone, and the use of new and/or different vocabulary. Specifically, and uniquely looking at v. 5 alone: the use of the word field (*sadeh*), which is not found in the first creation myth when speaking of the creation of the plants, is used here to convey this author's interest in the produce of the field, that is, agriculture. It is a marked feature of this second creation account. All of the earth's plants are referred to in relation to the field. It represents a secular, agricultural perspective and interest. Furthermore, the use of the term "field" foreshadows this author's interest in man as an agent for tilling these fields and as essentially defined vis-à-vis these produce producing fields (below).

The use of the expression *ba'arets*, "in the earth," when referring to the creation or nonexistence of the plants is unique here as well, and represents a different syntax and more poetic style than the more erudite and formulaic style employed by the author of the first creation account who repeatedly employs *'al ha'arets*, "upon the earth," when writing about the creation of the plants. The use of the verb "to grow" (*tsamah*) is also unique to the second creation account and once again accentuates this author's interest in the produce of the field, the rain, and the manpower required to grow it.

Finally, a new but most significant word is introduced in this second creation account when referring to the earth, *'adamah*—in contrast to the first creation account's use of *'erets*. This not only introduces this author's first among many puns and etiologies, but it is employed here to once again accentuate this author's central argument in his creation story—that man (*'adam*) is intricately attached to and essentially defined by the ground or earth (*'adamah*), from which he was fashioned. It is an etiological tale meant to provide, in fanciful storyteller fashion, the origin of man, and by extension man's relationship to the produce of the field. Both thematically and otherwise, this is a colossal difference from the claims of the author of Genesis 1:24–27, where man's (and woman's) creation is divorced from the earth!

All of these stylistic differences—and I've only noted them for v. 5 here—are unique characteristics of the second creation account alone. Conversely, the expressions and vocabulary found in Genesis 1:11–12—"vegetation yielding seed," "fruit trees producing fruit of its own kind," "seed of its own kind," and "trees producing fruit whose seed was in it"—are unique to the first creation account alone, and reflect this author's erudite and formulaic style and thematic interests.[22] These differences should not be neglected or interpreted away in willy-nilly fashion. Rather they should be embraced and understood. We could continue along these lines noting many more stylistic and thematic differences throughout the remainder of Genesis 2 if space permitted.

In sum, I hope my readers start to perceive that each creation myth was shaped by a variety of different factors. The first proceeds with a formulaic and ritualistic rigor, thematically and linguistically, presenting the creation of the then visible world in an order and fashion that is easily perceivable. Here in Genesis 2, on the other hand, the creation of man and then plants follows a rationale set by this author and his agriculturally oriented worldview. Creation does not proceed on any spatially or temporally ordered grounds as our first account does, but rather on etiological and thematic grounds with an eye toward linguistic wordplay and etymologies. It's a secular storyteller's creation account, not that of an elite priestly guild.

Genesis 2:6–7—Yahweh Molds an Earthling

In Genesis 2:5 we saw that the author of this creation story could not have Yahweh create the earth's vegetation until the two initial conditions necessary for their existence and growth were first established—a water source and a man. Thus the dry, barren earth that we were presented with in v. 5—one that was unable to support produce and vegetation—is immediately transformed in the following verses with the appearance of a mist that

22. A comprehensive list of the first creation account's unique features and vocabulary are enumerated and discussed in ch. 2.

swells up from the earth in v. 6, thus providing irrigation, and the formation of the man in v. 7, thus providing the labor needed to work the field's
produce.

> But a mist went up from the earth and watered all the face of the
> ground, and god Yahweh molded (*yatsar*) the man (*ha'adam*), clay
> from the ground (*ha'adamah*), and blew into his nostrils the breath
> of life and the man became a living being (*nephesh hayah*). (Gen
> 2:6–7)

The two initial conditions needed for the creation of plants are in
these verses now contended with: a water source and a man. It is only now
that this narrative can present the creation of plants and this specifically
takes the form of the planting of the garden of Eden. Thus every tree and
produce pleasant to the sight and good for eating in this garden has both
its water source to fertilize them (vv. 10–14) and the man "to till it" (v. 15).

Man's creation, its chronological placement in the narrative, the manner through which he is created and the reason why, the fact that only a
man in the singular is created, and the elemental material from which he is
created are all vastly different from man's (and woman's) creation as it was
presented in the first creation account. And as we saw in the case of the first
creation account, so too here: this account of man's creation was shaped by
the cultural concerns, worldview, and beliefs of its author.

Man's relationship to the earth is the central and predominant theme
in this second creation account and it is presented in several ways. Right
down to the creation of his very bones, man is defined in relationship to
and in the same terms as the earth! This is not only vastly different from the
views and beliefs of our first author, but completely negates and contradicts
them. From the perspective of the culture that shaped our present author's
attitudes and perceptions about man, the creation of man could not have
been drafted in any other way than by presenting him as a creature of the
soil, a thing of the earth—an earthling in a very literal sense. This is brought
out in several different ways.

First, v. 5 already foreshadows the conclusion of this etiological tale
explaining how it came about that man must procure his livelihood by
working the ground by initially referring to the absence of man in relationship to the absence of the earth's produce. In other words, before the
creation of man himself, the author of this text has already subtly suggested
that the ground, its produce, and man are all intimately connected together.

Second, unlike the author of our first creation account, this author utilizes a new and different vocabulary word for speaking about the earth or the ground—in Hebrew *'adamah*. Obviously the introduction of this term fits this author's purpose in presenting man (*'adam*) as a product of the earth (*'adamah*). By contrast, of the ninety-six times that the term *'adamah* appears in the Pentateuch alone, only six of these are found in the Priestly source! Moreover, the priest who penned Genesis 1 only uses the term as part of one unique expression, which we do indeed find in this author's creation account as well as this same author's flood narrative—"every creeping thing of the ground (*ha'adamah*)."[23] Thus not only does our second author, the Yahwist, introduce a new vocabulary word into his narrative for the purpose of defining man's essence, but he also employs this term in a different sense than that used and understood by our first author. Again such differences should not be neglected; they are more than differences of word choice. They reflect differences in cultural perspectives, worldviews, and even ideologies.

Third, in drastically different terms and imagination, cultural context and perspective, the author of this creation account portrays the man, Adam, being formed or molded (*yatsar*) from the ground (*'adamah*). Again, this is not just a difference in word choice, but a complete about-face in cultural and religious perceptions and ideas from those presented in the first creation narrative. Not only is man (and woman) *not* formed, molded, or crafted in the first creation account and presumably by Yahweh's hands, but the verb *yatsar* is *never* found in anything that the author of the first creation account, the Priestly writer, has ever written! It is an older term and one that was frequently used in the prophetic literature to speak of Yahweh as a potter who fashioned man, the clay of the earth, with his hands like a potter forms objects on his wheel.[24] So both the word and what the word denotes are utterly absent in the first creation account. That is, it would have been unthinkable to the author of the first creation account.

Lastly, the very fact that the author of this second creation account, and only this author, depicts man (*'adam*) being molded from the ground (*'adamah*) represents *this author's* unique views and beliefs—that man was not only created from the ground, but his very essence or being is defined both linguistically and substantively by the very same term and material as the ground! Man is in essence and in language of the ground. This is more

23. Gen 1:25; 6:20; 7:8; 9:2; Lev 20:25. See ch. 2 for a fuller treatment.
24. Isa 45:9; 64:8; Jer 18:4–6.

than a simple play on words for our author. Rather it helps to define man as intricately and essentially of the ground. It explains, in fanciful terms, the origin behind this author's cultural truth—why man ('adam) must procure his livelihood by working the ground ('adamah), and at that a cursed ground (Gen 2:5, 15; 3:17, 23). There is more to be said here in regards to man's relationship to the animals, which are also of the ground ('adamah).

In conclusion, none of these themes, ideas, and culturally formed beliefs about man, and only man, are present in the first creation account nor the mind of its author. They are unique to the second creation account and the aims and views of this author only. In fact, as I stressed earlier, the author of the first creation account purposely distances the creation of man and woman from the earth, from the animals of the earth, and from the manner in which the animals of the earth are created. By contrast, the author of the second creation narrative explicitly and purposely presents the fashioning of man ('adam), and only man, in relationship to the earth ('adamah), and, as we shall see, also in relationship to the fashioning of the animals of the earth. In sum, the author of the first creation account's presentation of the creation of man and woman together, male and female in the image and likeness of the creator deity, and apart from any etiological understanding of man only as a thing of the earth, is an explicit attempt to rewrite this older Yahwist creation story, with which he disagreed.

Finally, and again, contradictory to the first creation narrative, the author of the second account has a very specific reason for not presenting the creation of woman with that of man. And this has to do with this author's interest in etiology, wordplay, and how he and his culture perceived the essential natures of man and woman separately. For the fact of the matter is that for this author the origin of woman, unlike that of man (and his animal companions), is not of the soil! As we shall see, contrary to the author of Genesis 1:1—2:3, this author was writing an etiological tale with the express goal of representing and explaining the unique origins and essences of man and woman separately!

Genesis 2:18–20—Man and the Animals from the Ground, Woman from Man

In radically contradictory fashion to the creation of man (and woman) in the first creation account, when all is said and done in the second creation account, the substance from which man is made and that which he essentially becomes are shockingly no different than what is said about every other animal in this creation narrative.

> And god Yahweh molded (*yatsar*) the man (*ha'adam*), clay from the ground (*ha'adamah*), and blew into his nostrils the breath of life and the man became a living being (*nephesh hayah*). (Gen 2:7)

> And god Yahweh molded (*yatsar*) from the ground (*ha'adamah*) every animal of the field and every fowl of the skies and brought them to the man (*ha'adam*) to see what he would call them. And whatsoever the man called every living being (*nephesh hayah*), that was its name. (Gen 2:19)

In Genesis 2:4b–24, and only in this creation account, the essential nature of man, in both language and substance, is defined no differently than that of the animals. Both are molded (*yatsar*) by Yahweh from the ground (*ha'adamah*), and both are defined as living beings (*nephesh hayah*). Even after Yahweh blows into man's nostrils the breath of life, he still merely becomes no more than that which the animals are also defined as: a *nephesh hayah*!

Of course, our author purposefully created this connection and has a specific reason for doing so, as we shall see. But presently it needs to be stressed just how radically different and contradictory this image of man's creation is from the Priestly writer's image of man and woman's creation together in the image and likeness of God.

As previously noted, the author of the first creation account purposefully crafts the creation of man and woman in opposing terms and image to that of the animals of the earth. Only the animals of the earth, each created by their kind, are referred to as *nephesh hayah* in this creation account. This author's aim was to suggest that man and woman, unlike the animals of the earth, were made in the image of the god(s) and are consequentially more than mere *nephesh hayah*, living beings made after their own kind. By stark contrast, in the second account this label, "a living being" (*nephesh hayah*), is seen as man's crowning definition. And furthermore it does not distinguish him from the animals who are also *nephesh hayah*! This is a shocking negation of the views and perspective of the Priestly creation account, whose aims were to emphatically distinguish mankind's essential substance and mode of creation from that of the animals of the earth—not so for the Yahwist's creation account.

In fact, none of these themes—indeed arguments—are present in the second creation narrative, and on the contrary a set of opposite themes and arguments are made with reference to the creation of man, the animals, and lastly woman. It would do us well to listen to this author's specific arguments and point of view, rather than subordinating them to the claims of the first creation account and thereby neglecting them all together. Thus, whereas the first creation myth presents the creation of man and woman in different terms and image to the creation of the animals of the earth, the second creation account, by contrast, purposefully designates man, and only man, and the animals no differently—*nephesh hayah* formed of the *'adamah*. Furthermore, man and the animals are depicted on the same plane: the animals are each presented as potentially suitable companions for the man. They are seen as man's assistant helper (*'ezer*) or counterpart (*neged*) in this and only this creation account.

Why then did the author of this creation myth present man and the animals in similar terms and essences, that is, made of the same stuff? What was his message? And why didn't he include the creation of woman at this point in his narrative?

It should readily be perceivable by now that the Yahwist was quite the talented storyteller, and for the most part his stories, or those he himself inherited, were crafted to convey specific messages. We have already explored the rationale behind his presentation of man as substantively molded from the ground (Gen 2:6–7). This not only provided the Yahwist storyteller with a nice play on words, *'adam* from *'adamah*, but also explained from his cultural perspective why man is intrinsically attached to working the ground in order to procure his livelihood. Thus the Yahwist's stories have an etiological purpose; that is, they explain the origins of current customs, worldviews, and beliefs.

The story about how god Yahweh fashioned animals from the ground, the same essence from which man was made, is also an etiological tale, whose conclusion is to be found in the story of the creation of woman and the material from which she was made. It is a fanciful story explaining how man finally ended up with a woman as his life's companion and not an animal!

Genesis 2:18 specifically claims that god Yahweh molded the animals from the ground *so that* the man would not be alone, and *so that* he would have a counterpart or helper, that corresponded to his own being. Since man in both essence and name is of the earth, *'adam* from *'adamah*, it was only natural that a suitable counterpart for man be sought from the same substance and essence. Thus Yahweh fashions the animals too from the *'adamah* with the sole purpose of bringing them to the man so that he might *recognize* his own essence as it were among these potential suitors. We might again pause and note that this etiological story outright contradicts not only the order of the creation of the animals in the first creation account, but more significantly the manner and the reason for their creation as well. This narrative detail our author consciously created in order to construct a narrative explaining why man's life-partner is not found among the animals of the same essence as himself, but rather in another being, not yet created—woman. This story ends by claiming that Yahweh *could not* fashion from the ground a fit companion for man. He must now fashion man's companion not from the *'adamah*, the substance from which man was created, but from the substance of man himself!

> And god Yahweh caused a deep sleep to fall upon the man (*ha'adam*) and he slept. And he took one of his ribs and closed up flesh in its place. And god Yahweh built the rib which he had taken from the man into a woman (*'ishah*) and brought her to the man. And the man said: "This now is bone from my bones and flesh from my flesh. Accordingly she shall be called woman (*'ishah*) because from man (*'ish*) she was taken." (Gen 2:21–23)

The point behind the creation and naming of the animals in this second account is to give an account of woman's creation, who contrary to the animals, is the perfect fit/companion for man. There is additionally not only wordplay going on in this account, but also the presentation of a culturally formed perspective that accentuates the essences from which man, animals, and woman were all created, and therefore how each one's being defines them and their relationship to one another: man is essentially tied to and defined by the ground whence he was molded, *'adam* from *'adamah*, and woman is essentially tied to and defined in relation to man whence she was "built," *'ishah* from *'ish*.

This was a consciously constructed narrative on this author's part and represents a radically different cultural perspective and worldview than that presented in Genesis 1:27, where man and woman are both created together in the likeness and image of the divine. It may even be argued that the later sixth-century BCE Priestly writer who wrote what is now the first creation account vehemently disagreed with this earlier portrait which essentially defined man as of the earth, and woman as of man. Instead, the message of the first creation account and its author is that man and woman are essentially defined by the fact that they are both equally images and likenesses of the divine! These are radically contradictory and competing creation accounts of man and woman. Anyone seeking to harmonize these two different messages dilutes each one and neglects each author's unique perspectives and beliefs, valuing their own modern beliefs *about these texts* above the unique beliefs and messages expressed by the independent authors of these texts.

Finally, both accounts of the creation of man and woman serve as an etiological story explaining the origins of matrimony. This is more apparent in the second creation account. Why does man eventually marry woman? Our text responds by saying that it is because woman was substantially and essentially made from man's flesh. "On account of this a man (*'ish*) shall leave his father and his mother and adhere to his woman/wife (*'ishah*), and they shall become one flesh"—that is, as they originally were and still are! The first creation account gives a radically different answer. It is because God created mankind (*'adam*) as both male (*zakar*) and female (*neqebah*) together.

CONCLUSION

We have now seen that being honest to the texts of Genesis 1:1—2:3 and 2:4b–24, their historical and literary contexts, and the beliefs and views expressed therein has revealed that these two creation narratives were penned by different authors—an elite educated priest of the sixth century BCE and a secular storyteller of an older generation. Furthermore, both of these authors perceived and experienced their world, its nature, and its origin in radically different ways and thus produced radically different creation narratives. This conclusion, moreover, neither depends on the reader's persuasions nor beliefs. It is drawn from an honest and objective reading of the texts and the beliefs and worldviews expressed therein. Neither is this conclusion influenced or prejudiced by later reader-oriented theological interpretive frameworks that dictate beforehand what these texts allegedly are and how they ought to be read. Rather, these conclusions were uniquely drawn from the texts, what *they themselves* reveal about their own compositional natures and the beliefs and worldviews of their authors. This is studying the texts objectively, on their terms, and independent of the subjective views and beliefs of later readers. In sum, the texts of Genesis

1:1—2:3 and 2:4b-24 themselves reveal that the depiction of the origins of the world and of man and woman in both accounts were shaped by different and even contradictory cultural perspectives and beliefs about the nature of the world and of man and woman.

Each text also discloses that these differing authorial and cultural beliefs were legitimated by presenting them as the beliefs and views of the god of each one of these compositions. In other words, one of the literary techniques employed by ancient scribes was to place their beliefs, perceptions of the world, and even ideologies on the lips of God in the texts that they themselves composed. The god of their texts, in other words, is a literary creation. This observation is also drawn from being honest to what the texts themselves reveal about their own compositional nature and the literary conventions employed by ancient scribes in composing their texts. More will be said about this in the forthcoming chapters.

Thus any Creationist, Fundamentalist, or for that matter any individual who claims that they believe in the creation narrative(s) of Genesis is just not being honest to these texts, their authors, and their unique beliefs and messages. First, as we have seen, Genesis 1:1—2:3 and Genesis 2:4b-24 each express competing and at times contradictory messages, beliefs, and worldviews about the origins of the world and of man and woman. One cannot believe in both. Second, the beliefs and worldviews represented in these ancient texts each represent culturally accepted "truths" about the nature of the world and its origins as each of these ancient cultures perceived and experienced their realities. Our twenty-first-century beliefs and perceptions, not to mention scientific knowledge, about the nature of the world and of men and women are radically different from those depicted in both of these ancient texts. Thus in professing belief in the creation account(s) of Genesis, Creationists reveal that they value their own beliefs *about* the texts over and above the competing beliefs and messages expressed in the texts themselves. For these Creationists it's not about the texts and the beliefs and messages expressed therein; rather, it's all about their own beliefs and agendas and how they can legitimate them by disingenuously appealing to these ancient texts. It's a rhetorical appeal, not a substantive one as the texts themselves clearly disclose.

Chapter 2 builds upon these conclusions by providing a larger perspective of the beliefs and worldview of the author of Genesis' first creation account by examining in greater detail the larger composition that this author wrote, which scholars conveniently label the Priestly source.

2

The Seven-Day Creation Account
and the Priestly Writer

The seven-day creation account that now opens the Bible at Genesis 1:1—2:3 originally existed as the beginning of a once independent scroll centuries before Israel's ancient texts and traditions were collected and redacted together to form the Bible as we now have it. This scroll was written by an elite priestly guild sometime during the sixth century BCE, and it is for this reason that scholars have come to label it as the Priestly source.

The aims of this chapter are to point out some of the textual data that have led to this discovery, and to paint a larger portrait of this author and his priestly guild's worldview, religion, and even ideology through an examination of the central ideas and beliefs found in the rest of this once separate body of literature. It is my hope that this broader awareness will provide readers with the proper context in which to understand and even appreciate the meaning of Genesis 1:1—2:3 as its author originally intended.

THE REDACTION OF THE PRIESTLY SCROLL

The original Priestly scroll, which was composed during the sixth century BCE by a guild of priests who traced their lineage back to Aaron, is now spread across the first four books of the Torah, from Genesis to Numbers. The separation of this original Priestly scroll into smaller units of text was done in large part to accommodate other texts and traditions from an earlier period of Israel's history when scribes living in the fifth century BCE sought to compile a new edition of Israel's past by redacting the sixth-century Priestly scroll together with these older texts and traditions. It has even been demonstrated that the Aaronid priests who wrote this scroll did so to modify or even replace how the story of Israel's past was recited in these older traditions and to interject their own worldview, beliefs, and ideology into this new retelling. In the end, however, both these earlier traditions and this sixth-century Priestly scroll were redacted together to produce, in the words of the fourth-century scribe Ezra, "the Torah of Moses that Yahweh had commanded" (Neh 8:1).

It needs to be mentioned that this type of editorial activity was common among the literature of the ancient Near East. Scribes regularly copied, modified, and even rewrote the traditions that they inherited, and new compositions and even variant traditions were simply amended onto preexisting scrolls. Modern readers unfamiliar with how the literature of the ancient Near East, the Bible included, was composed, copied, and transmitted, and by whom and for what purposes, often object hostilely to the idea that the Bible is a redacted collection of previously existing traditions, many of which were written by rival guilds and scribal schools over hundreds of centuries, and which represent competing and even contradictory theological views and ideologies. Nonetheless, the textual data that support this claim are overwhelming, and frankly quite convincing.[1] The Bible *is* a collection of once independent scrolls and codices which, although now bound together, preserve variant traditions, competing worldviews and theologies, and even contradictory law codes, all of which were redacted together centuries after their compositions and labeled "the Holy Book" by a later generation of readers who had their own interpretive agenda and beliefs about the nature of these texts. Unfortunately this knowledge has been slow reaching the public, even though it has existed in academic circles for over two centuries now and has been repeatedly confirmed through the close reading and meticulous study of the Hebrew text and its ancient Near Eastern literary context.

With regard to the compilation of the scroll that would eventually become the book of Genesis, stories and traditions from ancient Israel that

---

1. See esp. Baden, *Composition of the Pentateuch*; Blenkinsopp, *Pentateuch*; Campbell, *Sources of the Pentateuch*; Carr, *Reading the Fractures of Genesis*; De Pury, *Le Pentateuque*; Doorly, *Laws of Yahweh*; Friedman, *Bible with Sources Revealed* and *Who Wrote the Bible?*; Knohl, *Divine Symphony*; Levine, *Numbers 1–20*; Levinson, *Deuteronomy*; Schniedewind, *How the Bible Became a Book*; Smith, *Priestly Vision*; and my forthcoming *Understanding Bible Contradictions*.

talked of creation, for example, were redacted together in the same place in this new retelling of Israel's past. This is exactly what we saw in our close reading of Genesis 1 and 2 in the previous chapter. Faced with preserving both the earlier eighth-century Yahwist creation account and the later sixth-century Priestly account, a later redactor decided, quite logically, to preserve them both side-by-side with the more majestic and optimistic seven-day creation account coming first. Contrary to the assumptions and prejudices of modern readers, the redactor's concern was not with eliminating competing and contradictory narratives; rather his concern may have been just the opposite—safeguarding Israel's variant and competing traditions!

At any event, this same editorial procedure was adopted for variant traditions and stories about the Flood, Abraham, Israel's covenant traditions, Joseph, Moses, the Exodus, the crossing of the Sea of Reeds, the giving of the law at Sinai, the golden calf incident, and on and on. All of these stories were variously told by different traditions of different dates and provinces, and for the most part these different "tellings" were preserved together at a later date to form a new narrative of Israel's past. In this manner the Priestly scroll was combined with earlier texts and traditions; or as some of my colleagues prefer, these earlier traditions were cut-and-pasted into the Priestly scroll.

Scholars have labeled these earlier traditions the Elohist and Yahwist traditions. The Elohist preserves traditions and stories from northern Israel before its fall in 722 BCE, while the Yahwist is a collection of many of the same stories, but which were recited differently in southern Judea, often with minor variations in narrative details or theological emphases. Today, in the Bible as it has come down to us, all three of these once independent sources have been stitched together to form the composite narrative that now extends from Genesis to Numbers. The book of Deuteronomy is its own unique textual tradition which was amended to this newly formed narrative, the JEP text, at a later date.

THE PRIESTLY SOURCE AS IT NOW STANDS

The Priestly source, which once existed as a separate individual scroll, now makes up the largest portion of the Pentateuch and is by far the most represented of the four Pentateuchal sources. It is the Priestly source that provides the main voice and interpretive framework for the first four books of the Torah. Its creation account not only opens the book of Genesis, but its formulaic inserts of genealogies, dates, land settlements, and covenant passages provide a chronological framework to the older JE material throughout Genesis and into the book of Exodus. It is not until the book of Exodus, however, that we find large portions of Priestly texts. Exodus chapters 25–31 and 35–40, which detail the construction of the sacrificial institution and the consecration of the Aaronid priesthood, are entirely from the Priestly writer. All of the sacrificial legislation and purity laws in the book of Leviticus are likewise from the pen of this priestly guild, and approximately 70 percent of the book of Numbers as well. In fact, excluding Exodus 32–34, which is a compilation of JE material, the literature spanning Exodus 25:1 to Numbers 10:28, including the entire book of Leviticus, is all from P! That is, a total of fifty consecutive chapters of Priestly material now occupy the central position of the Pentateuch. Excluding the book of Deuteronomy, the Priestly source makes up over 50 percent of the first four books of the Pentateuch: approximately 17 percent of Genesis is from P; 43 percent of Exodus from P; 100 percent of Leviticus is P; and 70 percent of the book of Numbers was written by P. Its presence is more than twice the size of any one individual source. Yet ironically, at least for modern readers, the Priestly literature and its author's aims and theology are the least known of the Pentateuchal sources.

One reason why the Priestly literature is not known to its modern readers is because of its meager appearance in the book of Genesis, which is the book of the Pentateuch that receives the most attention from modern readers, and conversely the prevalent disinterest among modern readers in the book of Leviticus, the core of the Priestly text. Even though Genesis opens with the Priestly writer's creation account, which does make a formidable impression, this writer's central concern with ritual, sacrifice, holiness, issues of purity, contamination, blood, and festivals and holy days, is barely perceptible in the limited context of his creation account. This is compounded by the fact that the Priestly creation account is often read separately and divorced from the rest of the Priestly corpus. This, as we shall see, is a mistake.

Besides P's creation account, other priestly passages now preserved in the book of Genesis include: P's version of the flood story which now exists interwoven with the older Yahwist version;[2] a set of genealogical records;[3] and most importantly this author's covenant passages, which were originally composed to amend, or perhaps even replace, the older Yahwist covenant passages, both of which were preserved side-by-side by later scribes.[4] From these meager appearances it is clear that this priestly guild had a vested interest in genealogies, dates, and covenants.[5]

The book of Exodus, on the other hand, starts to present a fuller picture of the Priestly writer's agenda. The most significant variations to the older traditions that the Priestly writer makes in his retelling of the stories now preserved in the book of Exodus are: the revelation of Yahweh's name for the first time in human history to Moses (Exod 6:2–10); the insertion of Aaron's genealogy (Exod 6:20–25) and a heightened significance of Aaron's role, even above that of Moses, throughout the Plague and Exodus narratives. Exodus 12 introduces the first cultic legislation of the Priestly writer, the Passover observance, here presented as a commemorative rite. This is now preserved side-by-side with the older Elohist Passover tradition.[6] The Priestly writer was also compelled to rewrite the crossing of the Sea of Reeds story, and the quail and manna traditions. But by far the largest additions to the earlier JE material by P include lengthy inserts into the Sinai tradition. For example, the Priestly writer added instructions for the building of Yahweh's tabernacle (Exod 25–31), and then gave a detailed account of its construction (Exod 35–40), which served to introduce the sacrificial institution and the Aaronid priesthood—that is, our author's guild. It is here that the Priestly writer's main agenda comes into greater focus. Creation, covenant, and cult are all brought together. We will explore these connections below.

The book of Leviticus presents the core of the Priestly writer's religious program, centered around the sacrificial cult which was officiated over by

---

2. In the combined PJ flood narrative as it now stands, these verses were originally part of the Priestly scroll: Gen 6:9–22; 7:6, 8–9, 11, 13–16, 21, 24; 8:1–2a, 3b–5, 7, 13a, 14–19; 9:1–17 (see Friedman, *Bible with Sources Revealed*, 42–47).

3. Gen 5:1–32; 10:1–7, 20, 22–23, 31–32; 11:10–32; 12:4b–5; 25:7–20; 26:34–35; 35:23—36:30; 46:8–27.

4. Gen 17:1–27; 28:1–9; 35:9–15; 48:3–7. See my forthcoming *Understanding Bible Contradictions* for a thoughtful analysis of how and why the later Priestly writer rewrote these older Yahwist covenant passages.

5. David Carr's work is invaluable in these respects. See his *Reading the Fractures of Genesis*, 78–113.

6. Compare Exod 12:1–20 and 40–49 (P) and Exod 12:21–39 (E).

the Aaronid priesthood. The opening chapters (Lev 1–7) were originally a private manual instructing the Aaronid priesthood in the proper performance of Yahweh's sacrifices. It was clearly an elitist text written for Aaronid priests only. The remainder of the legislation contained in the book of Leviticus focuses on ritual and ethical laws meant to separate the pure from the impure, clean practices and behaviors from those that were deemed unclean, and to safeguard both the camp's and the people's holiness against impurities. The importance of ritual and ethical separation and holiness cannot be overstated. It coincides with one of the central theological tenets of the Priestly guild—namely, that Yahweh dwelt in the tabernacle among the people. Thus all ritual and ethical impurities and uncleanliness threatened the deity's holiness and his presence in the community, and therefore needed to be immediately expiated by means of sacrifice. The whole sacrificial institution spearheaded by the Aaronids functioned to maintain, and reestablish when necessary, the holiness and purity of the camp where Yahweh dwelt by expiating and atoning for all unintentional sins—that is, unintentionally coming into contact with an impurity. According to this priestly guild, the sacrificial cult preserved the boundaries, holiness, and order that God established at creation. We will explore these connections in more detail below.

The book of Numbers continues with many of these same Priestly concerns, but additionally includes: more settlement records, this time associated with the tribal organization of the camp; a census of all males over the age of twenty; and a working itinerary for the scattered JE material in the larger context of the wilderness narrative. The latter half of the book of Numbers evidences Priestly legislation of a later period in an attempt to amend or rewrite previous laws now found in the book of Leviticus. Again, and in accord with ancient Near Eastern literary conventions, many of these variant laws were simply amended onto the same scroll.

STYLE, VOCABULARY, AND MESSAGE

Unlike the Yahwist and Elohist sources where scholars still debate whether or not they were once separate identifiable texts prior to their redaction, there is no doubt about the existence of the Priestly source. It is clearly identifiable by its unique style, vocabulary, and message. This is largely due to the fact that the Priestly literature was written by a single elite and very well educated guild, a priestly school which held fast to specific unswerving religious and cultic convictions, and had a language of its own for expressing those tenets. Thus, it's not surprising that we find an overabundance of cultic language and a style reflective of ritualized formulaic expressions in this corpus of literature.

The unique vocabulary employed by this Aaronid priestly guild is quite revealing in and of itself. At this body of legislation's core is its central figure, Aaron, who is mentioned approximately 260 times. This is remarkable when we note that outside of the Priestly source, Aaron is mentioned only forty-one times in the older Elohist tradition, and a mere four times in Deuteronomy! The Priestly literature's focus on Aaron, the Aaronid priesthood, and the sacrificial cult is even more pronounced when we compare this writer's vocabulary with other Pentateuchal sources. The term for "sacrifice," for example, appears fifty-five times throughout P, while only eleven times in E, and merely six times in D. The tabernacle, the central sacrificial institution for this Aaronid-led cult, is mentioned in P over a hundred times, while nothing is said of the tabernacle in any other Pentateuchal source. The word "priest," which not surprisingly gives this source its title, appears 270 times in P, while making a meager fourteen appearances in D! These are not just differences in word choice and vocabulary, but in the whole concept and purpose of religion as perceived by these two authors. The Aaronid priests of the Priestly source defined religion in terms of the sacrificial cult and, not surprisingly, their own priesthood. The Deuteronomist, on the other hand, defined religion in vastly different terms.

Other terms appearing frequently throughout the Priestly source, while not at all or marginally in other Pentateuchal sources include the word "holy," which is found ninety-one times in P and only nine times in D. The term "separate," as to separate the holy from the common, appears seventeen times in P and only five in D. "Be fruitful and multiply" is a unique Priestly expression occurring twelve times in P and nowhere else. The expression "Yahweh's glory" appears thirteen times in the Pentateuch, twelve of which come from P. The term "chieftain" appears sixty-nine times in the Pentateuch, sixty-seven of which come from P. And the word "congregation"—a favorite of P's—appears more than one hundred times throughout the Pentateuch, all from P. In addition to terminology, concern for priestly matters such as blood, impurity, sexual taboos, cultic festivals, the separation between holy and profane, distinguishing between clean and unclean foods, impure skin diseases, contamination, washing and hygiene, bodily emissions, the Sabbath, the observance of Yahweh's holy festivals, and the avoidance of blood and corpses are all concerns highlighted by our priestly author(s).

As is apparent from this brief summary of expressions and cultic emphases, the Priestly source rightly merits the title given it by academics. This once independent scroll clearly reflects the concerns and worldview of an ancient priestly guild.

THE SEVEN-DAY CREATION ACCOUNT AND THE REST OF THE PRIESTLY SOURCE: STYLISTIC AND THEMATIC PARALLELS

The creation account now preserved in Genesis 1:1—2:3 shares numerous stylistic, thematic, and religious characteristics with the rest of the Priestly corpus. Many of these features are unique hallmarks of the Priestly writer and his guild and are found nowhere else in the Pentateuch. It's time we looked at some of these features.

On stylistic grounds, Genesis 1:1—2:3 displays the hand of a well-educated and meticulous writer. This is immediately apparent in this writer's ritualistic attention to detailed expressions, language, and specific vocabulary that, as we shall see, are only found in the Priestly source. But even more impressionable is his repetitive and orderly style, which displays the mind of an individual who thinks in ritualistic terms: everything must have its proper place, order, and purpose. This pedantic and repetitive style comes across in this author's interest in organization, genealogies, chronologies, and other stylistic features such as his use of chiasmas and redundant noun-verb combinations, such as those already present in Genesis 1: "swarming-creatures swarming" (*sherets sharats*), "flying-creatures flying" (*'oph 'uph*), "creeping-creatures creeping" (*remes ramas*), and "seed-sowing seed" (*zara' zera'*). None of these stylistic features are found in the Yahwist creation account (ch. 1).

Additionally, this author's use of formulaic repetitions, spatial and temporal organization patterns, lists, and genealogies are readily apparent in other passages penned by this same author. Take a close look at the ritualistically detailed and repetitive style employed in Exodus 25–31 and 35–40, or Leviticus 1–7, 11, 13–15, 18, 23, or Numbers 1–4, 7, 26, 28–29, 31, and 33. All of these passages were penned by the same priestly guild and its particular style is not found any where else in the Pentateuch. This is not the secular storyteller style of the Yahwist, filled with word puns,

folklore etiologies, and place name etymologies. This is the style of an educated elite legalist, a priest. Furthermore, in every place where we find this
style employed, we also find the same themes, religious concerns, ideology,
and cultic worldview of the Priestly guild responsible for writing these and
similar passages. In other words, it's not just the style, the name of Israel's
god, or the specific religious beliefs and concerns that have enabled scholars to identify the Priestly source, but rather it is the convergence of all of
these features together, over and over in dozens and dozens of passages
throughout the Pentateuch.[7]

More specifically, there are a number of words and expressions found
in Genesis 1:1—2:3 that only occur in the Priestly source. The Hebrew verb
"to separate" or "to divide," for example, which appears five times in the
Priestly writer's creation account, is found a total of seventeen times in the
Priestly corpus, and conversely only five times in other non-P Pentateuchal
sources. This word choice is significant in this corpus of literature since
the primary task of the priests was to distinguish and divide between the
pure and the impure, the sacred and profane, in matters of the cult, human
activities, objects, bodily emissions, and even spatial and temporal borders.
It reflects this priestly guild's unique set of beliefs and worldview. Certain
things by their very natures are to be kept separate.

The word for dry land (*yabbashah*) is an identifiable Priestly marker. It
is not only used in Genesis 1:9–10, but also in this priestly writer's version
of the crossing of the Sea of Reeds story—yes, there are two once separate
versions—in Exodus 14.[8] This is revealing because the same story as recited
by the earlier Yahwist uses the Hebrew *harabah* which also means "dry
ground" in both his version of the Flood story and the crossing of the Sea
of Reeds story. In other words, while J consistently uses *harabah* for "dry
ground," P uses *yabbashah*.

---

7. See Friedman's discussion of this in his Introduction to *Bible with Sources Revealed*.

8. Besides the Priestly and Yahwist versions of the Flood now stitched together in
Genesis 6–9 (see n2), the Sea of Reeds tradition in Exodus 14 is another classic example
of a later editorial combination of the once independent Yahwist and Priestly sources.
Read the original Yahwist version where Yahweh drys the sea-bed by blowing back the
sea all night with his breath in verses 19b, 20b, 21b, 24, 25b, 27b, 30–31; and the more
commonly known Priestly version of Moses parting the sea with his rod in these verses:
21a, 21c–23, 26–27a, 28–29 (Friedman, *Bible with Sources Revealed*, 143–44). You'll
notice that both stories are continuous whole narratives on their own, each of which
employs their own set of unique words and images.

The noun *miqweh*, a "collection" (1:10), is unique to the Priestly source occurring once in Genesis and in only two other passages in the Pentateuch, both penned by P.

The Hebrew word translated as "by their kind," which appears ten times in the Priestly creation account alone, appears another twenty times in the Pentateuch, sixteen of which are found in other P passages. Notably, the term finds itself employed in P's dietary laws in Leviticus 11, and in only P's version of the Flood narrative.[9] More significantly we also only find in this author's creation account and flood narrative the lengthier and uniquely P expressions "every creeping thing of the ground by their kind" (Gen 1:25; 6:20; 7:14), "the animals (of the earth) by their kind," "the beasts by their kind," and "birds by their kind." These expressions are found nowhere else in the Bible, only in the Priestly source.

The Hebrew word for "lights" or "luminaries" in Genesis 1, *maʾor*, as opposed to the more frequent *ʾor*, is a term unique to P and occurs fifteen times in the Pentateuch, all of them in passages penned by P. *Raqiʿa*, the "domed expanse," is unique to P and other postexilic texts, as with the expression *tohu wabohu* (ch. 1). And as noted in chapter 1, out of the one hundred and sixty times that the word *moʿed* appears in the Pentateuch, only eleven of them are from non-P texts. The significance of this term, "fixed time" or "(festive) assembly" will be explored in chapter 3.

The noun *sherets*, "a swarm" or "swarming/creeping creatures," employed once in Genesis (1:20) is found fourteen more times in the Pentateuch, thirteen of which come from P. And the longer expression employing the verb, "creeping-creatures creeping" (*sherets sharats*), is only found four other times, all of which come from other P passages: P's flood (7:21) and P's dietary laws (Lev 11:41–44).

Likewise for the noun *remes*, "creeping-creature." It occurs three times in Genesis 1 and seven other places in the Pentateuch, all of them from P. Its verb form, *ramas*, occurs four times in Genesis 1 and ten other times in the Pentateuch, nine of which are from P. Moreover, the combined expression *remes ramas* is a unique Priestly innovation. It occurs once in Genesis (1:26) and four other times, all of which come from P. And as noted above, "every creeping-creature that creeps upon the earth" is an expression unique to P, occurring only here in Genesis, in P's flood narrative, and in P's dietary laws.

---

9. The other four places where this term is found are in the similar dietary code in Deut 14.

The word for serpent, *tannin*, occurs five times in the Pentateuch, four of which are from P. Significantly, P's version of turning Moses' rod into a serpent uses the same term, *tannin* (Exod 7:9–10), while the earlier Elohist version of the same story, now stitched together with the P text, uses the Hebrew *nahash*, "snake," in the same context (Exod 4:3).

The word for "image" which appears three times in Genesis 1:26–27 only occurs three other places in the Pentateuch, all of which were penned by the same author. Additionally, the specific expression "created in the image of God" is unique to P, occurring here in Genesis 1:27 and in one other place, Genesis 9:6.

The expression "male and female" as opposed to "man and woman," is also unique to the Priestly literature. In addition to appearing once in Genesis 1:27, it appears ten other times in the Pentateuch, nine of which come from P. On the contrary, the Yahwist tradition prefers to use "man and woman" in similar contexts, especially when referring to the animals being collected in the flood story. That is, while J uses "man and woman," P uses "male and female" exclusively and consistently.

The expression "be fruitful and multiply" occurs twelve times in the Pentateuch, all of them from P. The verb "to subdue" is also unique to the Priestly literature and other postexilic texts. And the verb "to have dominion over" occurs seven times in the Pentateuch, all from P.

The expression "bearing/sowing seed" (*zara' zera'*) is also unique to P. It appears four times in Genesis 1 and only three other times, all of which are from P.[10] In fact this redundant use of a verb and its noun—seed-sowing seed—is typical of the Priestly writer's style as we have seen elsewhere.

The term used for "food" (*'oklah*) in Genesis 1:29 is not only unique to the Priestly literature, appearing seven times in the Pentateuch, all from P; but it is also distinguishable from J's use of the word for "food"—*ma'akal* (Gen 2:9).

The verb "to consecrate" or "to make holy" obviously shares a unique place in any literature written by ancient priests. Out of the total seventy-five times this verb is used in the Pentateuch, sixty-three of them come from P. And the Hebrew for "work," *mela'kah*, is employed sixty-five times in the Pentateuch, fifty-six of which are found in other P passages.

These unique expressions and word choices reflect much more than just differences in style and language from the other Pentateuchal sources. Rather they reveal this author's unique mindset, religious beliefs, education

10. Lev 11:37; 26:16; Num 5:28.

and social standing, and even ideology. Furthermore, the Priestly writer's unique style and language is accompanied by a unique set of religious beliefs and themes only found in the Priestly source, some of which are already visible in Genesis 1:1—2:3.

The most prominent of these religious themes is undeniably this author's uncompromising views about the Sabbath and its observance. All of the Pentateuch's Sabbath laws, including the account of its consecration as a holy day by the creator deity at creation, were penned by the Priestly writer (ch. 3). For this author and the priestly guild he represented, the Sabbath was unconditionally part of the covenantal obligations of Yahweh's people, which was intricately connected to the cult and firmly grounded in the creation of the world. And it was this same author who composed a creation narrative illustrating why nonobservance was punishable by death[11]—because God himself created the seventh day as holy at the world's creation and even observed the Sabbath himself. Any nonobservance, therefore, was an affront to God *and his creation* (ch. 3).

The Priestly writer's adamant stance toward Sabbath observance rested on a much more profound and sacred view of the world. One quickly notices in this author's creation account the repeated emphasis on those things by which means time is measured and kept, the importance of which is only revealed later in the Priestly literature. For instance, P's creation account opens with the creation of light so that day can be measured, calculated, and separated from evening, and in fact so that the whole narrative progresses chronologically day by day leading to its climax in the seventh-day Sabbath observance. We are additionally informed that the luminaries and the sun and the moon were created "to divide the day and the night," and more importantly to serve "as signs and for the fixed times, and for the days and years." As we saw in chapter 1, the expression "fixed times" or "appointed festivals" is unique to the Priestly literature. These festival times, fixed by the movement of the moon, are specifically enumerated in Leviticus 23. They are Yahweh's "holy assemblies," many of which are decreed as eternal laws. We will explore their significance, especially in relation to P's creation account, in chapter 3.

Another thematic feature found in Genesis 1:1—2:3 that is shared with the rest of the Priestly literature is this author's illustration that order and goodness come through an act of separating the primeval elements of the world and keeping them separated. The primeval waters are kept at bay

---

11. Exod 31:12–17; 35:2; Num 15:32–36.

through the creator deity's creation of the sky—the solid domed expanse that keeps the waters above, above. Likewise the primeval waters below are also separated off and tamed through the creation of seas. This establishment of boundaries so that life may flourish is duplicated in the cult, where the central responsibility of the Aaronid priests was to distinguish between the pure and the impure, and to keep these spheres separate, or to reestablish their borders when breached. In terms of the legislation in the book of Leviticus, where the verb "to separate" is most pronounced, this act of separation entailed separating impure deeds, bodies, and even spaces from pure deeds, bodies, and spaces. Only through separating the pure from the impure could the boundaries and borders established at creation be maintained. This was the worldview that these priests lived in and endorsed.

Once again we textually see that no Creationist holds to this worldview and the beliefs predicated upon it. Rather these are the beliefs of an ancient elite priestly guild, and they were shaped by the specific needs and concerns of their historical circumstances. Such beliefs additionally highlight a concern prevalent during the exilic and postexilic eras when this corpus of literature was written: conceived as a holy people the Israelites were to separate themselves from the Babylonians, as well as the indigenous peoples of Canaan when the exiles returned to Judah, thus reinforcing Israelite identity. This belief in ethnic separation on the whole is also negated by our modern worldview and multiethnic global awareness.

Now let's take a detailed look at the specific beliefs and religious tenets endorsed by these priests in the larger body of literature they wrote.

CREATION AND THE CULT

The priests responsible for composing the creation account that now stands at Genesis 1:1—2:3 did so with an eye on the cult. This comes through most visibly in the priestly writer's ritualized and formulaic expressions, his insistence on order, boundaries, and classifications, his depiction of the creator deity in the role of a priest consecrating and blessing, and finally the consecration of the seventh day itself and the allusion to other holy days that were important parts of Yahweh's cult. Even more subtly, however, the priestly writer's presentation of creation as an act of separating and subduing the primordial elements so that an orderly good world can be established and sustained mirrors one of the fundamental functions of the cult—distinguishing and separating out from life's habitable sphere those elements that continuously threatened this good orderly world and the creator deity's presence in it. That the priestly writer perceived an intricate relationship between creation and the sacrificial cult over which he ministered is undeniable.

One of the ways that this was portrayed in the larger narrative that this priestly guild composed was to present the creation of the world and the erection of Yahweh's cultic institution mirroring one another, as the beginning and end of one continuous creative act. The creation of the world, the consecration and blessing of its seventh day, and the blessing of mankind in general find their counterpart in the creation of Yahweh's sacrificial cult, and the consecration and blessing of it and its priesthood. This together with the giving of the sacrificial legislation now preserved in Leviticus is the climax of P's narrative.

Not only is the tabernacle and Aaronid priesthood established and consecrated on New Year's day (Exod 40), an act commemorating creation, but the language employed by our author is used to subtly reference God's completion of his work in Genesis 2:1–3. As "God saw all that he had made" at the end of his creation, so too "Moses saw all of the work" which he did, namely, the construction and erection of the tabernacle and its components. And just as "God blessed the seventh day," so too "Moses blessed them." And just as "God finished his work that he had done," so too "Moses finished the work." These parallels were consciously created by our priestly writer to put the creation of the world and the erection of the cult in sync with one another. The cult, in other words, was seen by our priestly guild as an extension of God's creation.

First, the sacrificial cult functioned as the sole means on earth to connect the created world to its creator. Yahweh's altar was the meeting ground between man and God. In other words, the creator deity's presence and power in the world was visible through the sacrificial cult—a sacrificial institution, moreover, spearheaded and officiated over by the same Aaronid priesthood that wrote this text. In fact, this connection was so substantial that according to this priestly guild the creator god himself, Yahweh, actually resided at the center of this sacrificial institution, the tabernacle.

Second, the priests viewed and understood the cult and the duties of their own priesthood as an extension of God's creative work: separating, consecrating, and blessing.[12] The belief was that the sacrificial cult was the sole means of maintaining, and when necessary reestablishing, the created

12. See also Smith, *Priestly Vision*, 64–67.

order and boundaries of the world as God himself did so at its creation. So just as God's act of creating a sustainable and habitable world involved separating and keeping separate the primordial elements that threatened and continuously threaten life, especially as perceived by ancient Near Eastern peoples—flooding waters, desolation, barrenness—so too the priests' main responsibility in the cult was to maintain, and when necessary reestablish through sacrifice, the habitable sphere in which the people and their god dwelt by separating and keeping separate those elements that threatened life—disease, blood, death, etc. This was the primary purpose of the cult and, as we shall see, the focus of its legislation: to identify and separate from the sphere of life those impurities that threatened the community's well-being and holiness. In this regard, it was a continuation of God's creative act by keeping at bay those aspects of life that continuously threatened the created order, such as coming into contact with death, blood, bodily emissions, and other impurities. In other words, the priestly writer portrayed the creator god in his composition not only according to the terms that best exemplified and legitimated his own worldview and cultic concerns, but also according to the functions of his own profession as a priest: separating, consecrating, and blessing.

THE SACRIFICIAL INSTITUTION

Sacrifice was an integral part of the ancient world. The world needed sacrifices to keep it functioning properly, and according to our Aaronid priests, to even keep it as God created it! The issue, initially, was the problem associated with blood, particularly the shedding of blood. The answer was the institution of the sacrificial cult—Yahweh's tabernacle, altar, and priesthood.

Attentive readers have long noticed that in the Priestly writer's creation account mankind was initially designated to be vegetarians (Gen 1:29–30). It wasn't until after the flood, in P's version, that God okays meat for food (Gen 9:2–6), with, however, the restriction that its blood, conceived as the animal's life force (*nephesh*), could not be eaten. If one eats meat with its blood in it, our priestly author informs us, God will seek out that individual's blood, that is his life, as recompense!

A rather harsh sentence, but our priestly writer has a reason for placing these words on his god's lips, and that reason foreshadows one of the central functions of the sacrificial cult—to atone for the shedding of blood.

And that can only happen upon Yahweh's altar. Leviticus 17 lays this concern out most clearly.

> Any man from the house of Israel and from the foreigners that sojourn among your midst who will eat any blood, then I will set my face against that living being (*nephesh*) who has eaten the blood, and I will cut that individual off from among his people. For the life (*nephesh*) of the flesh is in the blood. And I have given it to you [to fling] upon the altar to make atonement for your lives (*nephesh*). For it is the blood that makes atonement for a living being (*nephesh*). (Lev 17:10–11)[13]

Thus in Genesis, before the altar and the sacrificial cult were established, whose function in part was to atone for the killing of an animal, even and especially for the purpose of consuming its meat, all that was commanded was that the blood not be consumed. But once the sacrificial cult is established, we see the broader concerns at play here for these ancient priests. It's not just the eating of blood that is forbidden, because it was considered the animal's life force, but the actual shedding of the animal's blood imparted "guilt" upon the individual who shed it.

> Any man from the house of Israel who slaughters an ox or a sheep or a goat in the camp or who slaughters it outside the camp and has not brought it to the entrance of the tent of meeting to bring forward an offering to Yahweh in front of Yahweh's tabernacle, blood will be imputed upon that man. He has spilled blood, and that man will be cut off from among his people. (Lev 17:3–4)

In the ancient world, one of the predominant reasons for sacrificing an animal was to consume its meat. This was especially so for those animals typically associated with other forms of sacrifice—oxen, calves, sheep, and goats. In ancient Israelite culture, if an individual or family wished to eat one of these animals, then they would have to sacrificially slaughter that animal, that is, bring it before Yahweh's altar and have the officiating Aaronid priest ritually prepare the animal. Parts of it such as its fat had to be sacrificially offered up to Yahweh. This was Yahweh's portion of the meal: "all fat is Yahweh's" (Lev 3:16–17; 7:23–27). Other parts, such as its blood, had to be flung upon Yahweh's altar to atone for the bloodguilt incurred by the individual who shed the animal's blood.

---

13. See also Lev 7:26–27: "And you shall not eat any blood in any of your dwellings, a bird's or an animal's. Any living being (*nephesh*) who would consume any blood, that same living being (*nephesh*) will be cut off from his people." (Cf. Lev 3:17)

We may wish to see in this a tacit realization—a view shared by priests throughout the ancient world—that it was necessary to repay life with life:[14] God seeks out that individual's life (*nephesh*) in compensation for, first the eating (Gen 9:5), and now the shedding of, the slain animal's blood, that is, its life force (*nephesh*). So Genesis 9:3–5 actually sets up a scenario that isn't resolved until the altar is established, whose purpose is to atone for bloodguilt by flinging the blood of the slain animal upon Yahweh's altar, symbolically returning the life force (*nephesh*) to Yahweh, and atoning for the bloodguilt incurred by the individual who killed the animal.

Note the theology at play here: the individual who sheds an animal's blood even and especially for the purpose of consuming that animal's meat, must atone for the life force he has just expunged—or else his life will be sought out as compensation by Yahweh (hinted at even in Gen 9:3–5). In order then to atone for that individual's life, which Yahweh seeks as compensation for the life just terminated, the animal's blood must be flung upon his altar. It is a ritualized act of returning the animal's life force back to God through his altar. And thus the one who had shed the animal's blood, that person, his life (*nephesh*) is atoned, his bloodguilt expiated. So one function of the sacrificial cult was to atone for bloodguilt—that is, the shedding of an animal's blood, and usually an animal intended for consumption.

Notice furthermore that there is no possibility of atonement for an individual who has shed the blood of another human being (Gen 9:6). An individual who has murdered another human being, that individual's life/blood is necessitated to repay for the life he has just taken, no exceptions.

> He that smites another shall surely be put to death. He is a murderer. The redeemer of blood shall slay the murderer upon encountering him. (Num 35:21b)

> Anyone who strikes a living being (*nephesh*), by the word of a witness the murderer shall be murdered . . . And you shall not accept a ransom for the life (*nephesh*) of a murderer who has been condemned to death. Surely he must be put to death! (Num 35:30–31)

We might surmise that the reason behind this has to do with the priestly writer's adamant stance against human sacrifice in general. The slaying of an animal automatically imparts bloodguilt onto the individual who shed that animal's life, and as a result his life (*nephesh*) is now required as recompense for the blood (*nephesh*) just spilt. To atone for his bloodguilt,

---

14. Ultimately this is the sense behind "a life for a life."

to ransom his own life (*nephesh*), the dead animal's blood must be flung upon Yahweh's altar: thus in effect, that animal's blood has just ransomed the life required of the individual that shed it. By the same token, atoning for the bloodguilt incurred by the shedding of a human life, and thereby ransoming the murder's own life, would likewise require that the blood of the slain victim be thrown upon Yahweh's altar. This however would have been utterly inconceivable and abhorrent to our priestly writers. Human blood on Yahweh's altar reeks of human sacrifice, and this was completely prohibited. Thus, a murderer was ineligible for atonement! "You shall not take a ransom for the life of a murderer; for he shall be put to death!" (Num 35:31).

We should additionally take a moment and let the text invite us into its priestly vision of the world, rather than attempting to interpret away this author's worldview and beliefs simply because they don't conform to ours or to those of later readers. The worldview portrayed here, as elsewhere in the Priestly corpus, was one shared by many ancient cultures. It is a pre-judicial worldview that works according to some rudimentary ideas about the world. An individual who has shed the blood of another human being automatically incurs bloodguilt. The same thing for an individual who has shed the blood of an animal, as we just saw. In this priestly worldview, blood is synonymous with life; it is the life force and as such was viewed as sacred. So we might even say that any shedding of blood, animal or human, is a crime against God according to this priestly worldview. In the case of the shedding of an animal's life force that crime, bloodguilt, is atoned through the placing of that life force upon Yahweh's altar. In the case of the shedding of the blood of a human, the bloodguilt that immediately falls upon the murderer, who is ineligible for atonement, is sought out by the "blood avenger." "The blood avenger (or redeemer of blood) shall kill the murderer when he comes upon him" (Num 35:19, 21). This idea of a blood avenger or Fury that seeks out the life of a murderer who has shed the blood of another is part and parcel to numerous ancient peoples in pre-judicial cultures.[15]

Once again (see ch. 1), we see that the world as it was perceived by ancient peoples, here ancient priests, and *their beliefs* about blood, about the shedding of blood, and about the function of sacrifice were transferred to the deity of that particular culture who then pronounces decrees and ordinances that more or less legitimate the worldview of the ancient priests

15. I'm particularly thinking of the ideas represented in Aeschylus' trilogy the *Oresteia*.

81

who wrote this text. The idea of a blood avenger is found in almost every primitive civilization, most notably the Greeks. Even in that culture the immediate need to avenge the slain blood of another human being was placed as an ordinance in the mouth of that culture's god. This is why a culturally contextualized reading of these ancient texts and their beliefs leads to the realization that, although we might believe in one or two common points or pithy philosophical statements in these ancient texts, we do not on the whole believe in the world created and portrayed by this author *and his god*, with its blood avenger, ideas of bloodguilt, and sacrifice. Anyone claiming that they do is just being dishonest and disingenuous toward the ideas and beliefs represented in these ancient texts.

Thus, we readily see two significant purposes that sacrifice served in the Aaronid cult: eating meat, which entailed slaughtering an animal and atoning for the bloodguilt incurred, and in more general terms as a mechanism for ransoming or atoning for an individual's life. In this priestly vision of the world, blood was the only means to atone for sin and specifically by splashing it upon Yahweh's altar. Much of this sacrificial theology remains in New Testament thinking, especially in how Paul interpreted the shedding of Jesus' blood on the cross.

This sacrificial theology of atonement by means of flinging the sacrificial animal's blood upon Yahweh's altar extends itself to expiating other "sins" besides bloodguilt. In the Priestly tradition, sin is usually articulated in terms of coming into contact with an impurity (see below) or unintentionally doing that which was prohibited. In fact the whole sacrificial system served as a means to expiate impurities when they befell the community at large, the land, or individuals specifically. However, this only included those sins committed by mistake or unintentionally—that is, unintentionally coming into contact with an impurity or impure body. All intentionally committed transgressions could not be atoned for. That individual was to be cut off from his people (Num 15:30–31)!

Sacrifices were also an integral part of keeping Yahweh's holy days holy. Both the Sabbath and the "fixed times" mentioned in Genesis 1:14 (see ch. 3) had their own accompanying sacrificial obligations that the priests were to perform. For example, every Sabbath, two unblemished one-year-old lambs were offered up to Yahweh as whole burnt offerings. Likewise, the Passover, the Festival of Weeks, Booths, and the Day of Atonement each had their sacrificial requirements.[16] Not withstanding, the fire on the al-

16. See Num 28–29.

tar was to stay lit day and night. And the *tamid*, which was a twice daily burnt offering of two lambs, was commanded to be kept every day. Many of these sacrificial offerings were deemed "eternal laws" by the Aaronid priestly guild. In part, these whole burnt offerings were a way of honoring the creator deity and connecting the deity with his creation. But specifically they were seen by our ancient priests as a means of feeding Yahweh! It was Yahweh who consumed these sacrifices as his daily food requirements.

Thus the sacrificial cult not only connected the world created in Genesis with its god through the altar, but more importantly it functioned to restore balance, purity, and holiness to the world by expiating sins, impurities, and bloodguilt incurred through the shedding of blood. It might even be advanced that the sacrificial cult functioned to help preserve the created world as God originally intended. Since at creation mankind was vegetarian, that meant that no bloodguilt was imparted upon mankind. After the flood, and without a sacrificial system to expiate sin, we might speculate that the priestly writers viewed the period from Noah to the consecration of Aaron as Yahweh's anointed priest as one that accumulated bloodguilt. Thus the sacrificial institution served to expiate sins or impurities, and thus restored the original state of holiness and goodness, the original state that merited the creator god's blessing at creation. The sacrificial cult, in other words, restored and kept the world as it was created.

THE AARONID PRIESTHOOD

Aaron is mentioned approximately 260 times in this body of literature identified as the Priestly source. This is significant given the additional data that Aaron does not appear in the earlier Yahwist source, is mentioned only forty-one times in the Elohist source, and a meager four times in the Deuteronomic source. Aaron, in other words, is the central most important figure for our Priestly writer. The reason for this is because this writer's priestly guild traced its lineage back to Aaron, whom—in a text that they composed—Yahweh selected among all the Levites to be his sole anointed priest in an eternal binding covenant.

> And bring forward to you Aaron, your brother, and his sons with
> him from among the children of Israel so that he may officiate as a
> priest for me . . . and you shall anoint them and fill their hand and

make them holy, and they shall officiate as priests for me. (Exod 28:1a, 41b)[17]

And the priesthood shall be theirs as an eternal statue. (Exod 29:9b)[18]

The Priestly source is the only textual tradition in the Bible that portrays Yahweh selecting and consecrating Aaron and his sons as his sole anointed priests. This selection, moreover, comes at the realization that this priestly guild's rivals, all non-Aaronid Levites, were demoted to mere servants of the Aaronids.

Bring forward the tribe of Levi and stand them in front of Aaron the priest. And they shall minister to him and they shall keep his charge . . . to do the work of the tabernacle . . . And you shall give the Levites to Aaron and his sons. (Num 3:6–9)[19]

The Levites, in other words, who were granted the priesthood in both the earlier Elohist source[20] and the book of Deuteronomy are here in this sixth-century Aaronid-written Priestly source demoted to non-priestly attendants of the Aaronid priests.

It is not surprising to learn, therefore, that this text was written by a priestly guild that traced its origin back to Aaron, or said more correctly, traced their exclusive right to the priesthood back to a story set in the archaic past that they themselves composed, wherein their forefather Aaron

17. Also Exod 40:13–15; Lev 7:35–36.

18. Also Exod 40:15, and Num 25:13 where Yahweh grants an "eternal covenant" to the Aaronid priesthood.

19. Cf. Num 8:18–19.

20. In the multi-sourced Torah as it now stands, the selection and consecration of Aaron and his sons as Yahweh's sole priests which happens in Exod 28:1–4, 41–43; 29:1–9; and 40:13–15, and thus also the demotion of all non-Aaronid Levites to servants of Aaron, is ill-placed. For sandwiched between these two Priestly passages—Exod 25–31 and Exod 35–40—is the Elohist's account of Aaron committing the "great sin," the golden calf incident, whose consequences led Yahweh to select the Levites as his priests, not Aaron and his sons! So in this multi-sourced text of the Torah as it now stands, in the Elohist text (Exod 32) we have Aaron committing the greatest of all the wilderness sins at the foot of the mountain, on account of which the Levites advance to the priesthood, while in the Priestly text (Exod 28–29; 40), at the same time on top of the mountain Yahweh is currently selecting and consecrating Aaron and his sons as his sole anointed priests and demoting all other Levites to servants of the Aaronid priesthood! This is merely one example where two conflating traditions were stitched together in the Pentateuch. See my forthcoming *Understanding Bible Contradictions*.

was selected by Yahweh to be his sole anointed priest! Much to the surprise of modern readers who lack knowledge about what ancient literature is, who wrote it, and what literary conventions were employed, this is properly what much of the literature of the ancient world was about—promulgating the particular ideology of the writer's guild! Thus contrary to what we find in this pro-Aaronid Priestly source, the pan-Levite text of Deuteronomy, for example, presents Yahweh selecting *all* Levites to be his priests.[21] This is just one example of how competing priestly guilds composed texts to legitimate their claims to the priesthood. Each guild, the Levites in general and the elite Aaronids in particular, vied for control, and each legitimated their positions by writing texts that used Yahweh as their spokesperson, placing their own ideology, worldview, and beliefs on his lips.

We should additionally keep in mind, as part of our task to properly understand these ancient texts, this composition's proper historical context, and conversely, its narrative setting.

The Aaronid priesthood came to power in the postexilic period when the Priestly scroll was most likely written. During this period, Israel was subjected to Persian rule and did not have a monarchy. The Davidic line ended with the Babylonian conquest, even though the pro-phetic literature produced during this time period reflected a longing and hope that Yahweh would restore the Davidic line of kings. At any event, it was the priesthood that reigned during this period, within which Israel

---

21. See Deut 18:1–5; 17:9, 18; 21:5; 24:8; 27:9; and 33:8–10. Readers should further note that when the seventh-century text of Deuteronomy was redacted together in the late fifth century BCE with the sixth-century Priestly scroll, these priestly rivalries and discrepancies become even more pronounced in this newly created redacted text. For in the Priestly text of Num 25:6–13 Yahweh is presented as making "a covenant of eternal priesthood" with the Aaronids through Aaron's grandson Phinehas. We are furthermore told that this happens after the mourning of Aaron's death in the sixth month of the fortieth year (see Num 20:28–29 and Num 33:38–39). This is P's text, written by Aaronid priests in the sixth century BCE. The text of Deuteronomy, however, whose narrative setting is just five months later on the eleventh month of the fortieth year (Deut 1:3), now presents Yahweh allegedly forgetting the covenant he just made five months earlier with the Aaronids, which in fact had been stressed throughout the last thirty-eight years of the wilderness period (see n25), and claiming that all Levites were eligible to be his priests! Again, this is not a portrait of God forgetting, but of competing textual traditions written by rival priestly guilds who used Yahweh as their spokesperson—as indeed was the common literary practice of scribes in the ancient Near East. Later these compet-ing priestly ideologies with their contradictory "Yahwehs" were redacted together and produced as it were this very contradiction that we are examining. Again, this is all part of recognizing and being honest to these ancient texts and the beliefs and ideologies of their once independent authors.

existed as a temple-state. The priests that came to power in the sixth to fifth centuries BCE were the Aaronids. To legitimate their right to rule as Yahweh's messiahs, his anointed priests, and to ward off potential rivalries, they wrote a text that sanctioned and authenticated their claim—the Priestly source. So while much of this scroll was written in the sixth century BCE—that is its historical context—the text's narrative setting was set in the archaic past, at Sinai. They then drew from the stories already embedded in Israelite tradition, but reshaped them with a focus on Aaron and an idealized version of the cult, which then served as a model for the Aaronid-led cult in the postexilic Persian period. Most importantly, this sixth-century priestly guild portrayed, in the composition that they penned, Yahweh selecting and consecrating Aaron and his seed as his sole priests at Sinai, while commanding all other Levites to serve them—a marvelous ingenuity of literary innovation!

My readers may be shocked to learn this. But quite frankly this is because of the unfortunate situation that exists today with respect to the absence of any education in the public realm about these ancient texts, the cultures that produced them, who wrote them, to whom and why, and the literary techniques employed by ancient Near Eastern scribes when writing to legitimate their beliefs, ideologies, and authority. These same literary conventions were employed by ancient Near Eastern scribes across the board. And since the Bible is a compilation of sixty-six different texts, the biblical texts themselves in comparative study bear witness to this very phenomenon. Many of the Bible's texts were originally independently written compositions by competing scribal guilds, priesthoods, and prophetic schools, whose texts were meant to legitimate that particular guild's or scribal school's position and authority by invoking Yahweh as its spokesperson. The same literary conventions are also employed in the New Testament, where Jesus becomes the spokesperson for the views and beliefs of each gospel writer. More than often, this legitimation came at the expense of having the deity condemn a rival guild's ancestor, as Aaron is in the golden calf story written by the Elohist,[22] or the Levites are in the Aaronid-

---

22. Again, this is easily discernable from studying the Bible's many texts individually on their own terms. So for example, in the present case the Aaronid-written Priestly source presents Yahweh selecting Aaron and his seed at Sinai as his sole anointed priests to minister his cult eternally (n20 & 25). Yet the pan-Levite written text of Deuteronomy presents Yahweh selecting all Levites as his priests (n21). And in the Elohist tradition of the golden calf story, whose setting is also at Sinai, and happening concomitantly with the selection of Aaron and sons in P (n20), Aaron is portrayed as bringing about Israel's

written Priestly source.[23] These were the literary conventions employed in the ancient world—placing the selection of one's guild and the degradation of that of your opponents in Yahweh's mouth in a text whose narrative setting was placed in the archaic past where Yahweh had selected that guild's forefather to rule as his sole anointed priest.[24]

"great sin" and as a result Moses selects the Levites to expiate this Aaron-caused sin and the Levites thus become Yahweh's priests! This Elohist story's historical context was most likely the ninth century BCE and it was written to condemn the Aaronid-led bull cults of Jeroboam I. The author of this story, a Levite or a scribe sympathetic to Levites, employs the same literary conventions used by the Aaronid author of the Priestly source. He composes a narrative set in the past that condemns the forefather of the priestly guild he is criticizing in the ninth century BCE—in this case, Aaron!

23. Num 3:5–10; 8:18–19.

24. The Pentateuch is not the only corpus of literature in the Bible that witnesses priestly rivalries. Both the postexilic prophetic traditions of Jeremiah and Ezekiel represent competing views on which priestly guild will be restored: the Levites in general (Jer 33:14–22) or only those of the line of Zadok, while all other Levites are to be demoted to servants of the Zadokite priests (Ezek 44:9–15). This textual legitimation of one's priestly guild against the claimants of their opponent's is also seen in the New Testament. Denying the "eternal covenant" and "eternal law" of this or that priesthood variously enumerated in the Hebrew Bible—whether that be the Aaronids (Exod 28:1–4, 41–43; 29:1–9; 40:13–15; Num 25:6–13; cf. 1 Chr 6:49; 16:39; 23:13), the Levites in general (Deut 18:1–5; 17:9, 18; 24:8; 27:9; 33:8–10; Jer 33:14–22; Mal 2:4), or the Aaronid Zadokites (1 Sam 2:27–30; Ezek 44:9–24; 1 Chr 15:11, etc.)—the author of Hebrews attempts to legitimate Jesus Christ as eternal priest based upon a reading of an ambiguous verse in Ps 110:4. Furthermore, this author employs many of the same literary techniques in legitimating his own beliefs. Just as the sixth-century Aaronid priestly writer composed a text whose narrative setting was before the giving of the law in the book of Deuteronomy where Yahweh is seen selecting Aaron and his seed as his priests in a binding "eternal covenant," so too the author of Hebrews legitimates Jesus as high priest by using an earlier reference to Melchizedek as priest (Gen 14), who precedes the coming and selection of Aaron and his seed! So this writer doesn't compose a new text set further in the past from when his rivals were selected as priests, like our Aaronid priestly writer does, but he rather reinterprets texts that have already become authoritative and places Jesus' selection as priest at a time in the past *before* Aaron was selected. This is the same literary technique. All of these authors attempt to legitimate later beliefs and the selection of their group by God by retrojecting it/them into the past. This is how ancient writers subverted the literary traditions that were authoritative during their time period while presenting their innovation (their new text or their reinterpretation of an older text) as the hidden "true meaning" of the very literary tradition they were attempting to subvert. For an excellent read on how the author of Deuteronomy subverts the literary tradition that he inherits while presenting his new reinterpretation of it as the very tradition itself, see Levinson, *Deuteronomy*.

"YAHWEH'S" PRO-AARONID LEGISLATION AND ETERNAL LAWS

There are numerous other examples of pro-Aaronid legislation and a pro-Aaronid Yahweh that are only found in the Priestly source—all of which stand in sharp contrast to the pan-Levite legislation and pan-Levite Yahweh of Deuteronomy. Thus, in this Aaronid-written text, and only in this text, do we find "Yahweh" endorsing: the sole selection of the Aaronids as his priests and the demotion of all other non-Aaronid Levites as their servants;[25] the sole right of the Aaronids to officiate sacrifices; and therefore the sole right of the Aaronids alone to expiate and atone for sin;[26] the sole right of the Aaronids to enter the tabernacle;[27] the sole right of the Aaronids alone to touch Yahweh's holy objects;[28] the sole selection of Aaronid priests as judges;[29] the sole right of the Aaronids to be able to eat Yahweh's sacrifices;[30] the sole right of the Aaronids as the beneficiaries of the people's firstfruit offerings and donations;[31] and the sole right and privilege of the Aaronids to burn incense.[32] All of these Yahweh-decreed pro-Aaronid privileges are only found, not surprisingly, in this text written by priests who traced their lineage back to Aaron.

Additionally, all the privileges enjoyed by the Aaronid priests and their function as Yahweh's sole ministers were also legitimated through divine decree by presenting them as "Yahweh's eternal laws." In other words, the Aaronid priestly guild responsible for the composition of this scroll has Yahweh decree all of the following as "eternal law": the anointing of the Aaronids as Yahweh's sole priests;[33] the daily lamp that must be kept lit by the Aaronid priests;[34] Yahweh's show bread which must be displayed daily

---

25. Exod 28:1–4, 41–43; 29:1–9; 40:13–15; Lev 7:35–36; Num 3:5–10; 8:18–19 (*contra* Deut 18:1–5; 17:9, 18; 21:5; 24:8; 27:9; 33:8–10).

26. Lev 1–7, and the book of Leviticus in general. See also Num 15 (*contra* Deut 18:1–5).

27. Num 1:51; 3:10, 38; 18:5–7, 22.

28. Num 4:1–20 (*contra* Deut 18:1–8; cf. 1 Sam 6:13–19).

29. Exod 28:30; Lev 13; Num 5:16–28 (*contra* Deut 17:8–13; 33:8–10).

30. Lev 6:9–11, 19–22; 7:1–34; 10:12–15 (*contra* Deut 18:1–4).

31. Num 18:8–19; Lev 6–7.

32. Exod 30:7–8; Num 17:5 (*contra* Deut 33:10).

33. Exod 28:1–4, 41–43; 29:9; 40:12–15; Lev 6:15; Num 10:8.

34. Exod 27:20–21; Lev 24:2–3.

by the Aaronids;[35] the Aaronid priesthood's portion of the sacrifices;[36] the daily sacrifice and continual fire on the altar;[37] the washing of the Aaronid priests before they enter the tabernacle;[38] the prohibition of beer and wine for Aaronids before entering Yahweh's presence;[39] and all donations, first-fruits, and sacrificial offerings belong eternally to Aaron and his sons.[40] In other words, the whole care and legitimation of the Aaronid priesthood and the sacrificial cult as envisioned and officiated over by the Aaronid priests themselves are repeatedly highlighted as "Yahweh's eternal laws" throughout the very text that they themselves wrote! Moreover, these eternal decrees occur nowhere else in the Bible but in this text, the Priestly scroll.[41]

Again for readers unfamiliar with ancient Near Eastern literature—and that is most "readers" of the Bible—this is precisely what ancient literature did and was composed to do. Properly we would label this as propaganda—that is, literature written to endorse and in this case divinely authenticate the sole authority, ideology, and beliefs of its authors.

Numbers 16–17 displays the power of this literary technique. How does an elite priestly guild ward off rivalry claimants to the priesthood by its opposition? Simply create a story set in the archaic past where a rivalry claimant does arise against Aaron and present Yahweh punishing these rivals by commanding death to all those involved and to their families! The effectiveness of such compositions is undeniable. In the present case, this story presents Yahweh stating definitively that all claimants to the priesthood by non-Aaronid Levites will be punished by a swift death. This message is exactly what the Korah rebellion story was composed to accomplish by its Aaronid writers. Thus any rivalry or challenge to the Aaronids' sole authority to reign as Yahweh's anointed priests in the fifth century BCE was squashed by referencing this ancient story, which in the end was composed exactly for this purpose! The lesson this story conveyed is clear: "No

---

35. Exod 25:30; Lev 24:5–9.

36. Exod 29:28; Lev 6:11; 7:34; 10:15; 24:9.

37. Exod 29:42; Lev 6:6.

38. Exod 30:21.

39. Lev 10:9.

40. Num 18:8, 11, 19.

41. One may find sympathetic decrees in the fourth-century books of Chronicles, which also display the concerns of an Aaronid author, and the book of Ezekiel, which was apparently written by an Aaronid Zadokite priest.

outsider, one who is not from the seed of Aaron shall come forward to burn incense before Yahweh" (Num 16:40). Indeed, no one but a descendant of Aaron could even approach Yahweh's tabernacle, that is, the altar and sacrificial compound. "And you shall charge Aaron and his sons that they shall protect their priesthood, and an outsider who approaches [Yahweh's tabernacle] shall be put to death" (Num 3:10).[42]

This and other similar stories in the Bible are quite powerful and they were composed to convey a poignant if indeed disturbing message: that under no circumstances are non-Aaronid Levites to challenge the Aaronids' sole right to be Yahweh's priests. These are carefully crafted lessons created by an elite priestly guild whose sole purpose in composing these stories was to endorse, legitimate, and safeguard their own authority and ideology, and often against the views and claims of rival groups who also composed texts that did exactly the same or similar. This is how ancient scribes and guilds legitimated their views, authority, and even social positions in the ancient world. They wrote texts and stories which exemplified their views and beliefs, and authenticated them by presenting them as divine decree. This is all part of our objective reading of these ancient texts—namely, reading and understanding them from within the cultures that produced them, observing the literary techniques that went into their compositions, and faithfully reproducing the beliefs and views of their authors.

SACRED SPACE

One of the most prevalent theological tenets that this priestly theocracy held was that Yahweh dwelt among the people, in the inner most shrine of the tabernacle. And this tabernacle existed at the center of their encampment—a figurative expression for the temple in Jerusalem. "Let them make me a sanctuary and I shall dwell among them" (Exod 25:8).[43]

This theological conviction alone necessitated a strict ethical and ritual code that quickly expunged and expiated any and all impurities that came into the community—thus the Priestly legislation's strict adherence to purity and holiness. Since Yahweh dwelt among the people, both the community's space and land were conceptualized in differing degrees of sacredness. In fact, the very presence of Yahweh and his tabernacle dictated

42. Cf. Num 3:38; 4:15, 20.
43. Expressed also in: Exod 29:45; Lev 26:11–12; and Num 35:34.

a hierarchy of sacred space, as well as strict purity regulations for the people and the land.

At the center of this holy encampment stood the tabernacle compound itself where Yahweh resided.[44] As such this space was deemed holy. It was the most sacred place in the community, and the inner most shrine where Yahweh resided was deemed the holy of holies. Only the Aaronid priest could enter it. Even the tabernacle as a whole and the larger complex of the tent of meeting were only open to Aaronid priests. Only they had been consecrated, made holy, and so only they could approach Yahweh's dwelling. Death was decreed to any non-Aaronid who approached this sacred space[45]—in a text, we must recall, written by Aaronid priests.

Moving down this hierarchy, after the Aaronids there was the larger body of Levites who ministered to the Aaronid priests. They had been purified, but nevertheless were prohibited from approaching the tent of meeting or even touching any of its sacred components. Only the anointed Aaronid priests could touch the tent of meeting's equipment. Further from the center of the encampment were the people themselves, who were commanded to be holy precisely because of Yahweh's presence. And lastly was the land itself. Any impurity or sin that befell an individual or even the land (such as a dead animal on the land) needed to be expiated immediately since this impurity risked encroaching upon Yahweh's holiness and indeed contaminating the sphere of sacred space within which this impurity was found.

The view that Yahweh tabernacled among the people allows us to understand why the Priestly legislation in the book of Leviticus is emphatically concerned with laws that: (1) prohibit coming into contact with impure/unclean things or spaces, or committing impure/unclean acts; and (2) legislate in cases of a breach between the pure and impure, the clean and the unclean, what was sacrificially required to mend this breach and bring the individual or community back to a state of purity and cleanliness lest these impurities encroached upon Yahweh's dwelling.

We will see in chapter 3 that time too was divided into sacred and profane days, and that these demarcations, such as those for sacred spaces, also needed to be observed. They were an inherent part of the created world as viewed by these ancient priests.

44. This is described in Numbers 2–3.

45. Num 1:51; 3:10, 38; 17:28; 18:22.

THE PURE AND THE IMPURE: A PRIEST'S WORLDVIEW

Throughout the book of Leviticus, and especially in those chapters devoted to its laws and commandments (Lev 11–22), the role of the Aaronid priests is repeatedly defined by the phrase "to distinguish between the holy and the profane, between the pure and the impure." In fact, the whole priestly law code is presented as the very instruction (*torah*) for doing this. Its *torahs* are "to distinguish between the holy and the profane, the pure and the impure" in matters of: diet (Lev 11); women, i.e., menstruation and childbirth (Lev 12); skin diseases and afflictions (Lev 13–14); bodily emissions (Lev 15); sex and nudity (Lev 18, 20); miscellaneous matters (Lev 19); and issues concerning the Aaronid priesthood (Lev 21–22).

Thus according to the priests who composed this text, certain foods are unclean or impure; a woman's menstruation is impure; any bodily discharge or emission is impure; leprosy and other skin infections are impure; in fact diseases by their very nature are impure; any clothes or a house that comes into contact with the infectious is also unclean and impure. Anything that touches, for example, pork, a corpse, the blood of a menstruating woman—whether a bottle, a piece of clothing, a bed, the walls of your house, etc.—also becomes contaminated and impure and must be purified through washing or simply discarded. Likewise, any individual coming into physical contact with a corpse or the blood of a menstruating woman also becomes impure. Exposing the nudity of one's relative is impure; homosexuality is impure; having intercourse with a menstruating woman is unclean; mix-breeding animals and different kinds of seeds is impure; eating a torn animal is impure, and so on. Moreover, any individual who has contracted an impurity (i.e., committed a sin) and does not expiate his impurity/sin through a ritualized washing *and* sacrifice officiated over by the Aaronid priest was irrevocably cut off and banished from the community.

In other words, taking this priestly literature at face value: Yahweh, God of the cosmos, believes that: all menstruating women are impure and need to be separated out from the community during their impurity; all persons with skin diseases and leprosy are likewise impure and must be taken outside the community; and ditto for those with any bodily emission, those who have come into contact with a corpse, those who have eaten rabbit, pork, clams, mussels, scallops, etc. And then of course there are the stricter penalties which "Yahweh" ordains of being permanently "cut off" from the community or even put to death for breaching the boundary between the sacred and the profane, the pure and the impure, in such matters as: eating blood or the fat of a goat, lamb, or cow; eating a sacrificial meal in a state of impurity; eating leaven during the Festival of Unleavened Bread; not fasting on the Day of Atonement; not observing the Day of Atonement, Passover, and especially the Sabbath; not being circumcised; partaking of the Passover while uncircumcised; having tattoos; practicing homosexuality, adultery, or bestiality; and knowingly committing any sin or transgression. Do these sound like the laws and beliefs of God, the creator of this world, or the views and beliefs of an ancient priestly guild?

The issue at stake here is not whether these views and moral legislation are no longer to be followed because they have been interpreted away by centuries-later reinterpretive endeavors that sought to impose new interpretive frameworks upon this ancient text. Rather, the issue is being able to properly identify and hopefully even understand this writer's and his priestly guild's worldview, beliefs, and culturally conditioned values, and how they were legitimated in the text he composed. Our goal, in other words, is to let this ancient text invite us into its perception of the world, not to impose ours or a later reading community's perceptions and beliefs about the world *and* God onto this ancient author's worldview and his portrait and understanding of God. Additionally, our goal is to acknowledge the literary conventions employed by ancient scribes. We already saw that the priestly writer's perception of the world and how he perceived and understood it as a priest living in the ancient Near East were transferred to the god of his text, from whose mouth this priestly worldview was represented and ultimately legitimated. The pure and the impure, the sacred and profane—this is how ancient priests saw their world, and thus the god in their text presents the world, its nature, and its creation, in these very same terms.

To reiterate, since this is such an important point, we are not talking about laws that later get reinterpreted away, as is often imagined to be the case by later misinformed readers. We are talking about unique beliefs and perceptions of the world that ancient peoples and cultures had, and the texts they composed to divinely legitimate their views of the world as they themselves saw and experienced it. When a later readership "interprets away" these ancient beliefs, moral legislation, and whole worldviews under the dictate of a later interpretive tradition that claims that these laws and beliefs are no longer valid because their world doesn't conform to these ancient ideas and beliefs, what they are tacitly doing is discarding this author's and his culture's beliefs and worldview—beliefs and a worldview that ultimately represented the views of the god of their composition as well. True, this ancient worldview and the beliefs predicated upon it are no longer valid ways to view and live in the world. They have become obsolete, but not because they are part of some divine plan as dictated by the theological precepts of a later interpretive framework, but because they represent the subjective and culturally defined beliefs and perceptions of an ancient people and culture that no longer exist. But to the authors who wrote these texts these were understood as cultural "truths" that reflected their perception and experience of the world. In fact, this perception of the world was understood by the author to be so truthful that he presented it as God's view! Later, and modern, readers of these ancient texts cannot just interpret this worldview away or deny the beliefs and messages of its author simply because his worldview and beliefs no longer conform to those of a later readership. What we can do—and are obliged to do I would argue—is to understand this priestly guild's worldview and belief system *on his terms* and from within his cultural context—not to interpret them away by imposing the terms of later readers, later historical and literary contexts, and later theological constructs.

For the priests that produced these texts, the pure and the impure, the sacred and the profane, represented *their* world—how they truthfully viewed the world at its essential nature. The pure and the impure were categorically and essentially inherent parts of the created world. The whole priestly worldview, in other words, boiled down to seeing the world in terms of what is sacred and what is profane, what is pure and what is impure. It is at root a worldview built on the sole belief that the world is divided into sacred bodies, sacred spaces, and sacred times (ch. 3). In this regard, our modern economic worldview is, literally, world's apart from the worldview, belief system, and values of the Aaronid priestly guild that wrote this text— values and beliefs which were ultimately presented from the mouth of their god, Yahweh. The demarcation of sacred space and the maintaining of that space were the only things that mattered in living life for this priestly clan, and by extension the Yahweh of its text. Moreover, the worldview presented here in the book of Leviticus is the exact same worldview we find hinted at in Genesis 1. It is a worldview representative of, and one which belongs to, the archaic past. No one today believes in it. And as responsible modern readers of these ancient texts we should acknowledge this fact as well as the unique beliefs and worldview expressed in these texts—not simply interpret them away.

Another unique feature of their worldview, which is also no longer shared nor believed by modern readers, is that impurity, that is, what was deemed impure, was conceived as a contagion. That is, individuals who came into contact with a corpse, menstruating women, or who became impure through the eating of pork for example, not only contracted the impurity themselves but they risked passing it on to others as well, and most dangerously risked contaminating Yahweh's holiness and his tabernacle.

A good example of the contagiousness of impurity, as envisioned by these ancient priests, can be seen in the rites of purification for the leper, for menstruating women, and for coming into contact with a corpse. In all these examples, the impurity contracted by the individual happens through causal contact or in one case just by being in the same room as the impurity itself.

The most contagious impurity by far was death itself. Numbers 19 illuminates, through the mouth of Yahweh, this priestly writer's culturally conditioned perception toward death: "Anyone who has touched the corpse of a human being who has died and does not expiate his sin [through the prescribed sacrifice] defiles Yahweh's tabernacle, and that person will be cut off from Israel" (Num 19:13). We are furthermore instructed that in the event that a human being dies in a tent, house, building, etc. anyone who enters that enclosed space and everyone found inside it automatically become impure for seven days and must also perform the necessary purification rite. Likewise, anyone coming into contact in the open air with a slain human body, or a corpse, or a human bone, or even a grave, also becomes impure for seven days. In other words, the beliefs of this priestly guild, presented as the very beliefs and worldview of Yahweh, dictated that in absolutely no terms could an individual come into contact with the dead, a part of a corpse, the ground of a buried corpse, etc. and not become impure. Death, blood, and diseases were all envisioned as impurities by this priestly guild, and these impurities were furthermore understood as airborn contagions! Numbers 35:30–34 relates that if a murderer, that is, one who sheds the blood of another, is not immediately put to death, because he has incurred upon him bloodguilt, then the whole land upon which that murderer resides is at risk of becoming polluted!

These, then, are the beliefs, values, and worldview of the elite priests who penned Genesis 1 and who lived in a world, it must be acknowledged, vastly different from our own. This is not *our* world! People who interpret these beliefs away under the misguided dictates of centuries-later re-interpretive frameworks are in fact tacitly consenting to exactly what I'm trying to demonstrate here: such individuals have implicitly asserted that these are not the laws that govern our world at large. Our world, its metaphysical makeup, is not constructed on inherently and divinely assigned natures of pure and impure. If the god of this two thousand five hundred year old text created a world where the seventh day was deemed and declared holy and consecrated, and menstruating women, blood, bodily emissions, diseases, certain foods, certain sexual activities, death, and even certain spaces were all declared impure, and yet we as a culture living millennia later and under a drastically different worldview and belief system disregard these demarcations between sacred and profane bodies, actions, time, and spaces, then what are we doing but unconsciously acknowledging that this is rather the views and beliefs of ancient peoples, not ours, nor even *our* God's! Is this the world that the god of modern-day Creationists created? It certainly is not. Then the next logical question to ask is: have our so-called Creationists created a new god to legitimate their claims and beliefs about *our* world, its nature, and its origins, since the Yahweh of the text that the author of Genesis 1 composed certainly does not! For the god of Genesis 1 legitimates a vision of the world and its creation that belongs to the worldview and belief system of the ancient priests who composed this text—not to those of its modern readers.

A WORLD WITHOUT SATAN, DEMONS, OR EVIL

Lastly, it must be mentioned against later theological worldviews more pronounced in the New Testament and among modern believers, that in this priestly worldview there was no concept of demons or Satan. These ancient priests, and their god, did not conceptualize their world in these terms. Rather, if we wish to speak of those "metaphysical" elements that were antagonistic toward Yahweh in the priestly worldview, we would have to limit it to the category of impurity itself.

The priest's world, as they perceived it, was demarcated by pure and impure bodies, actions, spaces, and even time. It was impurity itself that threatened the holiness of Yahweh; and it was the coming into contact with an impurity that was labeled as a sin in this priestly worldview. That is to say, in the whole corpus of literature that these Aaronid priests wrote there is no talk of Satan, demons, or even evil for that matter. The priests simply did not conceptualize their world in the terms that later readers did. In other words, these priests *and their god* did not believe what later readers came to believe!

On a broader scale, it must be borne in mind that the concept of an evil agent other than and apart from Yahweh is frankly a late development. There is no Satan, nor demonic forces that stand apart from nor are antagonistic toward Yahweh in the earliest texts of the Hebrew Bible.[46] Such ideas do not emerge in the Hebrew canon until the Hellenistic era under the influence of Persian religious beliefs. This is a fact contested by the biblical texts themselves and the views and beliefs of their authors. Biblical scholar and Hebraist William Propp explains:

> In most of the Hebrew Bible, God plays the role later Judaism reserves for Satan. *Ha satan* "the Adversary" first appears in early postexilic writings as an officer in Yahweh's angelic court entrusted with presenting human behavior in the worst light (Zech 3:1–2; Job 1–2). But when Judaism encountered Zoroastrianism, Persian dualism evidently attracted thinkers troubled by Yahweh's role in creating evil and misfortune. Beginning in the Persian period, various spirits—Belial, Mastemah, Asmodai, Sammael, the Evil Impulse, Satan—assumed the task of seducing humanity toward evil and launching attacks against individuals. For example, although it is Yahweh who tempts David into sinfully ordering a census (2 Sam 24:1), a later retelling (1 Chr 21:1) makes the instigator Satan. Similarly, while it is Yahweh who attacks Moses in Exodus 4:24, in Jubilees 40:2, the adversary is Mastemah. Even the command

---

46. Biblical texts written prior to the third century BCE, for example, present Yahweh in the role of what later gets attributed to Satan or an evil agent. Textual examples include: "Shall evil exist in a city and Yahweh has not done it?" (Amos 3:6); "I am Yahweh and there is no one else. I fashion light and create darkness; I make peace and create evil. I am Yahweh who does all these things!" (Isa 45:6–7); "Who makes a person dumb or deaf, gives sight or makes blind? Is it not I, Yahweh!" (Exod 4:11); "There is no god with me: I kill and I make life; I destroy and I mend" (Deut 32:39). All of these citations express a very specific belief held by ancient scribes—namely, that Yahweh was sovereign. Although today people pay lip service to this idea, they are a far cry from actually understanding what this means, and conversely meant to these biblical scribes. As a theological postulate "Yahweh is sovereign" means exactly what the citations above articulate. There is no other, no other metaphysical or spiritual being or agent, that produces evil, destruction, illness, etc. Yahweh is seen as the agent of all these things on both individual and national levels. This is what is meant by "Yahweh is sovereign." Again, this archaic view of the deity is not how our culture conceptualizes God, nor does it reflect what our culture believes about God.

that Abraham sacrifice his son (Gen 22:2) is, according to Jubilees 17:15–16, Mastemah's doing.[47]

None of these later developments and beliefs exist in the Priestly corpus. Rather, what continuously threatened Yahweh's realm and holiness according to our priestly writer were impurities and their contagious natures. There was only the pure and the impure, the holy and the profane. So questions of morality or ethics were subordinated to issues of purity and impurity. In this worldview, sin was committing an impurity, unintentionally coming into contact with an impure body, or refusing to observe Yahweh's holy days.

This priestly worldview, and the literature that endorsed and legitimated it, is not only at odds with our own twenty-first-century worldview, beliefs, and values—quite obviously, but this needs to be repeatedly emphasized against those who would suggest otherwise—but it is also world's apart from the worldview, beliefs, and values of the authors of what became the New Testament. We should not be alarmed by this; after all we're talking about the world as viewed—as created—by an elite priestly guild of the sixth and fifth centuries BCE and the world as seen through the eyes of secular writers living centuries later and in a radically different cultural context and worldview, politically, religiously, and metaphysically. One part of being honest to the texts of the Bible is acknowledging these differences and contradictory worldviews—not interpreting them away through the theological dictates of later interpretive traditions.

THE PRIESTLY WRITER'S COVENANTS

The Aaronid priests who composed the Priestly source have Yahweh decree a unique set of "eternal covenants"—unique because these covenants only exist in the Priestly source. They are the eternal covenant of circumcision (Gen 17:1–14), the eternal covenant of the Sabbath (Exod 31:12–17), and the eternal covenant of the Aaronid priesthood itself (Num 25:10–13).

These "eternal covenants"—circumcision, the Sabbath, and the Aaronid priesthood—are additionally never mentioned as Yahweh's covenants in any other textual source in the Pentateuch. Both the Mosaic covenant of Exodus 20–23 and that of Deuteronomy 12–26 present Yahweh proclaiming covenantal stipulations, but the three covenants of the Priestly

47. Propp, *Exodus 1–18*, 354.

source are never mentioned as covenants in these law codes. In the book of Deuteronomy, written by a different priestly guild, circumcision is *never* mentioned nor even acknowledged as part of the Mosaic covenantal stipulations! This is surprising since the book of Deuteronomy on the whole is a covenant text.

But the Priestly writer, writing later than both of these textual traditions, rewrote Yahweh's covenants—as circumcision, the Sabbath, and the Aaronid priesthood—and rewrote the Sinaitic law code, which now makes up most of the book of Leviticus. The importance placed on circumcision and Sabbath observance—unique identity markers of Jews in the ancient world—have also supported the claim that this literature was composed in the exilic and postexilic periods when these issues were of some importance in maintaining Israelite identity vis-à-vis the Babylonians themselves while the Israelites were in captivity or the indigenous peoples of Canaan when they returned to the land.

THE "DIVINE" PUNISHMENT OF *KARET*

As we saw above the expression "eternal law" is a unique lexicon of the Priestly source, and reflects those cultic elements that were dear to the Aaronid priests who wrote this text. These so-called divinely ordained eternal laws legitimated and substantiated the Aaronid cult, the Aaronid priesthood's sole right to minister to Yahweh, and even the Aaronid priests' religious privileges and social authority, all as they themselves perceived it.

Similarly, this Aaronid-written body of legislation also presented Yahweh decreeing stern punishments for any individual who failed to observe the "eternal laws" and "eternal covenants" expressed in this Aaronid-written text. So another unique feature of the Priestly source is its "divine" punishment of *karet*, that is, being "cut off." So in this corpus of literature "Yahweh" decrees that an individual will be cut off from his people, his covenant, and his land if that individual: neglects the eternal covenant of circumcision (Gen 17:14); does not keep the eternal covenant of the Sabbath (Exod 31:14); does not observe the festivals of Unleavened Bread (Exod 12:15, 19), Passover (Num 9:13), and the Day of Atonement (Lev 23:29–30); comes into contact with the dead and does not expiate this sin through a sacrifice (Num 19:13, 20); bootlegs holy oil or incense (Exod 30:33, 38); eats a sacrificial meal in a state of impurity (Lev 7:20–21); eats fat or blood (Lev 7:25, 27; 17:9–10, 16); slaughters or sacrifices an animal in the open field (Lev 17:4, 9); eats sacrificial meat more than three days after it was slaughtered (Lev 19:8); does not fast for the Day of Atonement (Lev 23:29); commits a number of sexual violations including exposing a relative's nudity, homosexuality, bestiality, and having sex with a menstruating woman (Lev 18:29; 20:17–20); performs necromancy (Lev 20:6); sacrifices a child (Lev 20:2–5); and last but certainly not least of all, knowingly commits *any* sin (Num 15:27–31)!

Once again, properly understanding what ancient literature is and specifically here the agenda of this elite priestly guild, we see that all these prohibitions and their punishment of *karet* are an expression of the beliefs and worldview of the Aaronid priesthood that penned this text, legitimated and sanctioned by presenting them through the mouthpiece of Yahweh. In their composition, in other words, Yahweh is used by the priestly scribe to endorse, by divine decree, the ritual and festive aspects of the Aaronid cult. None of these eternal laws which solely focus on the Aaronid sacrificial cult are found in Yahweh's mouth in any other textual tradition preserved in the Bible.[48]

"HE SHALL BE PUT TO DEATH!"

Although offensive to many people today, capital punishment was the norm throughout much of the ancient Near East. All of the commandments to exercise capital punishment in the Priestly source can also be understood as an expression of the culturally shaped views and beliefs of the elite priests who penned this text. Thus, we find that "Yahweh" condemns to death: anyone who murders another individual (Lev 24:17, 21; Num 35:16–21); anyone who desecrates or does not observe the eternal covenant of the Sabbath (Exod 31:14; 35:2; Num 15:35)—which most likely includes 99 percent of all of our so-called modern day Creationists; adulterers (Lev 20:10–13); a man who sleeps with another man (Lev 20:13); a man who marries a woman and his mother (Lev 20:14); a man who marries his brother's wife (Lev 20:9); having sex with an animal (Lev 20:15–16); the daughter of a priest who loses her virginity prior to marriage (Lev 21:9); profaning Yahweh's name (Lev 24:16); and any non-Aaronid who approaches Yahweh's dwelling (Num 3:10, 38; 18:22; 25:6–9).

The point of this study, once again, is not to interpret this priestly writer's worldview and belief system away through the aid of later theological

---

48. With the exception of other Aaronid-written texts such as the books of Chronicles.

frameworks just because they do not substantiate later beliefs about the world and about the text. But rather to see and understand them as they are—culturally formed perceptions and beliefs about the world that were substantiated by presenting them as the divine decrees of that culture's god. All the views, beliefs, moral legislation, eternal covenants and eternal laws with their divine punishment of being cut off or put to death, and what is deemed inherently sacred and profane, pure and impure, presented in this body of literature represent those of the priests who penned this text. It is not only *their* worldview—not ours—but it is the same worldview, depicted less explicitly, that is presented in Genesis 1. The priestly concerns for ritual purity, sacred spaces and time, holy days and the Sabbath so pronounced throughout the legislation that they composed can also be seen in the creation narrative that they composed. It's time we took a closer look at how sacred time was also created at creation and embedded into the very fabric of the created world according to this priestly guild and the creator god of its text.

3

Creation and Sacred Time

One of the most essential and defining beliefs of the priests who wrote the seven-day creation account was that the world at its creation was divided into sacred and profane time or days, that God himself created and set apart at creation specific days as holy, and that these holy days were discernable to mankind by the moon, which the creator deity created in part to serve as a sign to inform mankind when these sacred, holy days occurred so that they may be observed and kept holy forever.

These were the beliefs of our author, and they were shaped by an uncompromising religious worldview that stretched across the ancient Near Eastern basin and which was particular to how priests of this ancient landscape viewed and understood their world. Pure and impure, sacred and profane—these were the categories that defined the nature of the world for the Aaronid priests who wrote Genesis 1:1—2:3. And as we saw in the previous chapter, these categories extended themselves to defining spaces, bodies, human actions, and even time.

Imagine momentarily what it would be like to live in this priest's world, the world that he portrays his god creating. Imagine living in a world, society, community, neighborhood, that defined everything in terms of sacred and profane spaces, pure and impure bodies and human actions, and whose calendar system was set by the monthly position of the moon which signaled the arrival of specific holy days whose essential god-created natures could not be profaned. Imagine living in a society whose main concern was to avoid contracting impurity and thereby contaminating the sacred space in which this community resided. Imagine also a legislative system whose sole purpose was to establish laws that helped prevent against contracting impurities both individually and communally, that prescribed the necessary means to expiate such impurities when breaches occurred, and that decreed punishments for those who intentionally committed impure deeds, and this most certainly included profaning holy days by blasphemously working or doing common deeds during their occurrences. In short, *really* imagine living in the world that our priestly author has God create!

Quite frankly we cannot even begin to imagine such a world because these are not our beliefs! We do not view the nature of the world in these ritualized categories. When we go out into public, eat something, wear something, go to work, or do anything on any given day we do not think about whether what we're doing is pure or impure, a clean or unclean act, whether we've walked into an impure space or come into contact with an impure body, or whether it's a holy day or not. Even our use and understanding of such terms as "sacred" and "holy" have become diluted and secularized in comparison to how the priests who penned Genesis 1:1—2:3 understood these terms. We may use "sacred" to define the space of a church or the time of day of its worship, but these have merely become rhetorical nomenclature. For we don't, and wouldn't even think of, stopping menstruating women from entering church, or any public sphere for that matter lest their "impurity" contaminate us all, or much worse contaminate God's holiness! We don't inhibit individuals who have come into contact with corpses or sick family members, have open wounds, or have eaten pork, scallops, etc., from entering our so-called "sacred" spaces. We don't quarantine individuals with skin infections or exposed bodily fluids, and we certainly don't destroy all physical items—housewares, clothes, cars—that these "impure" individuals have come into contact with. We don't condemn individuals for eating what is holy to God: fat and blood. And finally, we don't put to death individuals who go to work or do any menial task on the holy Sabbath day, or for that matter fail to keep holy any of Yahweh's holy days, all of which are to be calculated—not by our manmade calendar—but by the calendar God created at creation for this specific purpose.

This is the Bible's creationism! And frankly speaking no one believes it, follows it, or conceives of the nature of the world and its origins in these terms, especially our so-called modern day Creationists. We do not live in a world that would even facilitate believing in these ancient priestly beliefs

and perceptions of the world. Nor do I see any of our modern day Creationists believing in these beliefs or arguing for their preservation, or in
broader terms even believing in the priestly vision of the world as presented
in Genesis 1:1—2:3 (ch. 1). Yet modern day Creationists would have you
believe that they believe in the world created in Genesis 1:1—2:3. In reality they merely feign belief out of ignorance about what this ancient text
actually says. This has already been textually demonstrated in chapter 1.
Indeed, our culture's way of perceiving, engaging with, and living in the
world are so radically different from what these ancient two thousand
five hundred year old beliefs represent that our worldview and theirs are
utterly incompatible and contradictory. Our own modern beliefs and scientific truths about the essential nature of the world *invalidate* the beliefs
and worldview held by the ancient priests who penned Genesis 1:1—2:3.
The very manner in which each and everyone of us lives our lives on a
daily bases invalidates these beliefs. No one in today's twenty-first-century
world believes, or could possibly even believe, in the beliefs and worldview
represented in Genesis 1:1—2:3. The textual data from this two thousand
five hundred year old text with its archaic beliefs about the nature of the
world (ch. 1), the scientific reality of the laws of our universe which has led
to the invention of numerous electronic toys and gadgets that facilitate our
lives, the empirical data of how we live our lives on a daily bases, and the
psychological data of how we perceive and understand our world all bear
witness to this fact. Anyone claiming that they believe in this two thousand
five hundred year old text, its beliefs, and worldview is merely feigning belief, and ultimately being disingenuous toward this text and what its own
author actually believed. More problematic, such belief claims are not only
disingenuous and misrepresentative of the belief claims actually made by
the author of this ancient text, but they also fuel staunch hypocritical and
uneducated opinions since one now claims to believe in something that he
or she actually doesn't believe in and on top of that knows nothing about to
begin with. Isn't it time our so-called Creationists started being honest to
these ancient texts, and ultimately to themselves as well?

GROUNDING THE HOLY SABBATH IN CREATION

All of the Torah's Sabbath laws,[1] including the account of its consecration
as a holy day by God himself at creation, were penned by the same author

---

1. Gen 2:2–3; Exod 31:12–17; Exod 35:2; Lev 23:3; Num 15:32–36.

or priestly guild—our Aaronid priests. Indeed the Sabbath itself has a much earlier origin than the writings of this sixth-century BCE priestly guild. It is found in the earlier Yahwist and Elohist traditions and even listed as a central part of both of these traditions' Ten Commandments:[2]

> Remember the Sabbath day, to keep it holy! Six days you shall labor and do all your work, but the seventh day is a Sabbath to Yahweh your god. You shall not do any work! (Exod 20:8–10)

But it was the Aaronid priests who composed a creation narrative that anchored this holy seventh day and its observance in the creation of the world.

> And on the seventh day God finished his work which he had made; and he rested (*shabat*) on the seventh day from all his work which he had made. And God blessed the seventh day and made it holy, because on it he rested from all his work which God created and had made. (Gen 2:2–3)

We should immediately notice that the Aaronid priest who composed this creation account has God *make* the seventh day, the day on which he rested from his work, holy. The Hebrew is a one word verb (*qadash*): "to consecrate," "to sanctify," or "to set apart as holy." Although I have translated this verb as it commonly appears in the majority of English translations, "made (it) holy," it might best be translated as "set (it) apart as holy" or "consecrated (it)." Indeed, the very fact that the text has the creator deity bless the seventh day and rest on it by extension "makes it holy." The seventh day *is* holy specifically because God had rested on it and in that resting he "made" it holy.

The point is that our author is claiming that the seventh day is holy, consecrated—and therefore must be kept that way eternally by respecting and observing its sacredness—precisely because the God of creation made it, or set it apart, as holy when he created the world. The Sabbath now becomes, under the plume of this priest's pen, an inherent part of the created world; the two are inseparable. The seventh day's holiness is embedded right into the very fabric of creation itself! This is our priestly writer's argument. This is his creationism.

We should also notice that although the creation of mankind is a climatic event in the Priestly writer's creation account, it is not the climax of

---

2. The Sabbath was so central that it was enumerated as part of both Ten Commandment traditions, the Yahwist's (Exod 34:21) and the Elohist's (Exod 20:8–10).

his narrative: the Sabbath is. The whole creation account moves toward and finds its resolution in the seventh day, which is additionally consecrated, blessed, and set apart as holy. In fact, the sole reason for having presented the process of creation in sequential days (day one, day two, day three, etc.) was to establish the fact that it was day seven that the creator deity set apart as holy. This was the initial framework upon which the priestly writer drafted his composition—a seven-day creation account that sanctified the Sabbath as a holy day of rest in its essence. It could not have been a one-day creation account as we find in the earlier Yahwist account (ch. 1), or a three-day creation account. It needed to be a seven-day creation account that, from the perspective of the priests who composed this account, legitimated once and for all the sacredness of the seventh day, the creator God's Sabbath, and thus also the absolute and unconditional eternal obligation to observe this day as holy, since the creator God established and consecrated it as holy in its essential nature when he rested from his creation.

The creation narrative, in other words, was pre-designed to answer the why and the how of the seventh day's holiness. Thus, observing the Sabbath day as God himself did becomes not just a law to follow, but rather a god-created inherent structure of the world itself. Observing and keeping the Sabbath is therefore observing and keeping holy the inherent nature of the world *as God created it and observed it himself!* This is the priestly writer's world, the world that he has his god create.

Again, we should note that not one so-called Creationist observes, keeps, nor believes in the world as created, observed, and believed by the god of Genesis 1:1—2:3. Their professed belief, in other words, is disingenuous, even hypocritical, and ultimately based on later reader-imposed traditions *about* the text, rather than the text itself and its author's beliefs and worldview.

MAKING THE SABBATH AN ETERNAL COVENANT WHOSE NONOBSERVANCE IS PUNISHABLE BY DEATH

Not only did the Priestly writer compose a creation account that grounded the origin of the holy Sabbath in God's creation of the world, but he also converted it into an "eternal covenant" whose nonobservance was punishable by death! Following the literary conventions employed by ancient scribes throughout the ancient Near East, this was legitimated and sanctified by presenting it as Yahweh's direct and final word on the matter.

And Yahweh said to Moses, saying: "And you, speak to the children of Israel and say: 'Surely you shall observe my Sabbaths, for it is a sign between me and you throughout your generations, to know that I, Yahweh, make you holy! And you shall observe the Sabbath, for it is holy to you. *Everyone who profanes it shall surely be put to death!* . . . Six days work may be done, but on the seventh day is a ceasing, a Sabbath, holy to Yahweh. *Anyone who does work on the Sabbath day shall be put to death.* And the children of Israel shall observe the Sabbath, to do the Sabbath throughout their generations, *an eternal covenant!*'" (Exod 31:12–16)

These are the words which Yahweh commanded them to do: "Six days work may be done, but on the seventh day there shall be to you a holy day, a Sabbath, a ceasing for Yahweh. *Anyone who does work on it shall be put to death!*" (Exod 35:1–2)

And it happened while the children of Israel were in the wilderness that they found a man who was collecting wood on the Sabbath day . . . And Yahweh said to Moses: "*The man shall surely be put to death!* All the congregation is to hurl stones at him outside the camp!" And all the congregation brought him outside the camp and they hurled stones at him and he died, as Yahweh had commanded Moses. (Num 15:32–36)

All of these passages were penned by the same writer or priestly guild that composed Genesis' seven-day creation account. And it is only in this corpus of literature, the Priestly source, that the Sabbath is mentioned as one of Yahweh's "eternal covenants," to be observed "throughout your generations." And only in P do we find Yahweh commanding the death penalty for any and all individuals who do not keep the sanctity of this holy day, grounded, as it now is, in the very fabric of the created world.

It is clear that the Aaronid priests who composed these passages were uncompromising when it came to Sabbath observances—so much so that they had Yahweh declare it an eternal covenant whose nonobservance was punishable by death, no exceptions! The Priestly writers also composed a story that exemplified this covenantal law and the severity of its nonobservance in the most trivial of matters. Numbers 15:32–36 recounts the story of a man who was caught collecting firewood on the Sabbath. Our author has Yahweh respond: "The man shall be put to death!" Period. No exceptions!

This story was created to convey a powerful, if disturbing, lesson: that even the most trivial of deeds—collecting firewood—was viewed as an intentional, blatant act of profaning that which God created as holy. Under no circumstance is any work of any sort to be done on the Sabbath. Any such violation would be punished with a swift death "as Yahweh had commanded."

Why was the death penalty unequivocally commanded, no exceptions, as the punishment for working on the Sabbath? What was it that made it so offensive to the priests who composed these passages, and, apparently to their god as well?

We actually have the answers to these questions, and they are found in this author's creation account: because the seventh day's holiness is an intrinsic structure of the created world, consecrated and even observed by the creator god himself when he created the world. Any nonobservance, therefore, not only failed to recognize the sacred nature inherent in creation itself, but it was also a blatant and deliberate act of blasphemy against the creator God *and his creation*. This is why our priestly writers take such an uncompromising stance on the matter.

For our Priestly writer, there was no escaping the holiness and sacredness of the seventh day. This was the day that God himself separated out from the secular and declared holy at creation. It is an intimate part of creation. That is to say, its sacredness and holiness is as much a part of the created world as the sun is! One cannot just interpret it away. Moreover, its sacredness is God's very holiness. The Priestly writer's thesis is that by not observing this holy day, one not only intentionally transgresses one of Yahweh's commandments, but more significantly this is a transgression of the worst degree since one has consciously and willingly elected to *profane creation itself* as well as the creator deity himself. How could there be a more severe crime than profaning God's creation?

This, then, was our priestly writer's argument; and death was seen as the appropriate response to such a blatant act of blasphemy—a blasphemy, it must be noted, committed on a weekly basis by just about every so-called modern day Creationist around the globe!

So again, how can anyone in today's society, with its radically secular conception of the world and secular culture, advocate and claim that they believe or follow the beliefs inherent in this ancient text with its priestly worldview? They simply cannot. Anyone making such claims is either ignorant about the text itself and what it says or is a hypocrite—or both. For our secular society, culture, values, worldview, manner in which we live and experience the world on a daily basis all invalidate the ancient beliefs inherent in this text. And, it might be added, rightly so! This was strictly speaking an ancient priest's worldview. Genesis 1:1—2:3 is an ancient priestly guild's creationism. It is not the creationism of modern day Creationists. This is not some outlandish subjective claim that I am making. Rather this is an objective claim being made by our object of study—the text of Genesis 1:1—2:3 itself! And it's about time Creationists started being honest to this text and the beliefs therein by acknowledging that they do not in fact believe in the beliefs and worldview represented in this ancient text.

NEGLECTING, ALTERING, OR INTERPRETING AWAY THAT WHICH GOD CREATED AS HOLY AT CREATION

Despite the claims of interpretive traditions forged centuries after the Priestly source was written, the argument that our priestly writer himself has painstakingly advanced in his composition of Genesis 1:1—2:3 serves as this section's title: that which God created in its inherent essence as holy at the world's creation cannot be neglected, abolished, altered, or interpreted away. That is to say, observing and keeping the Sabbath *is* acknowledging and preserving the world as the god of Genesis 1:1—2:3 created it! The Sabbath day is that part of the created world which the creator god created as holy. It is, as our author has Yahweh proclaim, "an eternal law," "an eternal covenant." This is our author's, and his god's, belief and perception of the created world. It cannot be altered or interpreted away. It can only be understood, and on the terms of its author—not those of later readers.

Modern so-called "readers" of these ancient texts, influenced by later interpretive frameworks, most notably those created centuries later by New Testament writers, regrettably miss our author's point or simply toss it in the wastebin. The priests perceived their world and believed at an elemental and essential level that the seventh day was categorically holy in its very nature, that God created it holy. This was a natural law, if you will, of the created world. This is why any and all nonobservances were punishable by death. Because an individual who failed to acknowledge and keep holy that which God created in its essence as holy when he created the world deserved to die. What greater blasphemy could there have been? These were the beliefs of the priests who penned Genesis 1:1—2:3. They are not ours, nor our culture's beliefs. Neither does our way of life substantiate these beliefs in anyway. Creationists simply feign belief when they claim that they believe in and adhere to the priestly creation account of Genesis 1.

To put this in perspective, particularly for my Christian readers who have been influenced by interpretive frameworks and agendas created centuries after our priestly text was written, to say that one no longer needs to follow the Sabbath or that the Sabbath is now abolished would be analogous to claiming that we no longer need to obey the law of gravity! That the law of gravity has been rescinded. We are no longer obliged to follow it!

Of course this is a ridiculous thing to say. But this is precisely the point that the priestly writer was attempting to make: as we perceive the law of gravity to be an inherent part, even truth, about the nature of the world and all bodies in this world are subject to its law, so too this was how the priests who wrote the creation narrative in Genesis 1:1—2:3 perceived the Sabbath. For the priestly writer this holy day was essentially and inherently a part of the very fabric of the created world itself, just as the law of gravity is for us post-Newtonians. One cannot interpret it away, or abolish it, or say that it no longer needs to be observed. Similarly, one cannot claim that the seas that the god of Genesis 1 created no longer need to be seas, or the sky no longer needs to hold back the waters above. One cannot change the beliefs and perceptions of our ancient author, how *he* perceived his world. This is being disingenuous to this ancient text and the beliefs represented therein. Our goal, rather, is to enter into this ancient priest's vision of his world and understand it—understand why he believed what he did and how he legitimated his beliefs. Being honest to *his* text and *his* beliefs, then, is realizing that they differ from our beliefs and scientific truths about the nature of the world.

This gets precisely to the point that we as a culture need to start realizing: we do not believe in the perceptions and beliefs about the nature of the world and its origin expressed in this two thousand five hundred year old text. We don't conceive of the world as essentially and categorically divided into sacred and profane time set by the creator God at creation. Moreover, as the text itself once again demonstrates, no so-called Creationist actually believes in this ancient text, its beliefs and *its creationism*. Rather belief is feigned due to lack of knowledge about what this ancient text actually says and lack of understanding why it says what it says. Being honest to the texts themselves, therefore, entails acknowledging the beliefs represented in these ancient texts, and likewise acknowledging that our beliefs and views about the nature of the world are radically different from those represented in this corpus of ancient literature. This ancient text and the views and beliefs expressed therein must, in other words, be understood on their own terms and from within their own worldview and belief system—not interpreted away by later readers, nor forced to fit into later scientific worldviews. This is simply holding our culture's beliefs as more important than those of these ancient scribes, and moreover at the expense of these authors' beliefs and worldview.

Today, the Sabbath is mere talk. The day is as profane as any other day. In fact, Christianity's insistence on interpreting away the Sabbath, on abolishing the creator God's "eternal covenant," an "eternal law" of the created world of Genesis 1:1—2:3, is an unconscious admission that the world and the beliefs about the nature of the world represented in this archaic text do not coincide with our knowledge and reality of the world we live in. The very act of interpreting away this "eternal law," in other words, is an admission that the worldview presented in Genesis 1:1—2:3 with its sacred time is not the world that modern Christian Fundamentalists and Creationists imagine *their* God to have made. The Bible's creationism *is not* the creationism of modern day Creationists! Our modern culture can comfortably interpret away the world as the god of Genesis 1:1—2:3 created it because no one really believes in it anyhow, which, we might admit, is only natural. The problem arises when modern groups, such as our so-called Creationists, out of ignorance about the text, its author, *his* beliefs, and *his* worldview, hypocritically profess belief in this ancient text with its ancient worldview. It's a belief that rests and relies on what later readers *have claimed about* this text rather than on the beliefs and worldview advocated in this ancient text itself by its author, and by extension its god!

Finally, even if Creationists wished to uphold the ancient beliefs presented in this two thousand five hundred year old text and keep the god of Genesis 1's holy day holy by observing the Sabbath on the seventh day, the problem is more pronounced since the god of Genesis did not make the seventh day holy according to a manmade calendar system! So these Creationist have also imposed our secularism and secular worldview upon the sacred worldview and beliefs represented in Genesis 1:1—2:3.

GOD'S CALENDAR WHICH HE CREATED AT CREATION

Honoring and keeping holy the days which the god of Genesis 1:1—2:3 set apart as holy requires knowledge about how the days were measured by this priestly guild—and its god. Part of that answer is discernable from the Priestly writer's creation account in Genesis. For like the Sabbath, the creator God also established and embedded into his creation a calendar as an inherent part of his creation.

In his creation narrative, our author has the creator deity proclaim that he is creating the heavenly luminaries not only "to distinguish between day and night" but also, and perhaps more importantly "to serve as signs for the fixed times." These fixed times or *mo'adim* were introduced in chapter 1 and are individually specified by our same Priestly writer in Leviticus 23. Being as literal as we can to the Hebrew, here are the *mo'adim* and how their occurrences were calculated according to the calendar which the creator God established through the creation of the luminaries.

- The Sabbath   on the 7th day
- The Passover   on the 14th day of the 1st (new) moon
- Unleavened Bread   on the 15th day of the 1st moon
- Horn Blast Assembly on the 1st day of the 7th moon
- Day of Atonement   on the 10th day of the 7th moon
- Festival of Booths   on the 15th day of the 7th moon

Of all the luminaries that the god of Genesis created on the fourth day of creation, it is the moon that serves as the preeminent sign indicating on what day from each consecutive new moon of the year Yahweh's holy festivals are to be observed. Thus, all of the holy days that God creates as part of his creation—the Sabbath and his fixed festivals—are discernable by the moon's position or phase. It is the moon, and particularly its creation as "a sign," which serves to identify on which days the creator God's holy festivals occur and are to be kept, eternally. Finally, the first day of each new moon was reckoned when the first crescent of the new moon appeared in the evening sky.

Once again, no Creationist follows this, believes this, nor advocates it, even though it is, according to the author who penned this text, part of God's creation! No Creationist observes these holy days which were established at creation as "eternal laws" by the god of Genesis 1, and certainly no Creationist observes these holy days or "fixed times" according to the calendar that this creator deity specifically created as part of his creation for the observance of these "holy assemblies," which were declared "eternal laws" by the creator god himself. The reason is: that despite their professed belief, they, and we as a culture, do not hold to these beliefs about the nature of the world. Rather, it must be realized that this calendar system and its holy days were part and parcel to the world as perceived by the ancient priests who penned this text. It is not part of our world, not part of the objective world, nor is it part of our culture's narrative about the world's creation. We simply do not believe this. Rather these are the beliefs of the ancient priestly guild responsible for composing this text. They are their culturally conditioned beliefs about the nature of *their* world.

In another Priestly passage we are told when exactly the year's first new moon appears. It is no coincidence that the New Year coincides with the exodus event, when Yahweh reveals himself to his people for the first time (at least according to the Priestly writer) and takes them as his people. The priestly authors conceived of the event as the beginning of the year.

> This moon is the beginning of moons [i.e., months] for you. It is the first of the moons of the year for you. (Exod 12:2)

Thus Exodus 12:2-6 and Leviticus 23:5—both from the Priestly quill—place Passover on the fourteenth day of the first moon or month. This first moon is the month of Abib, which was associated with the spring harvest. In other words, from the moon itself, which God created as part of the creation of the world to serve as a sign for his fixed holy days, all of Yahweh's holy days can be observed and kept holy. For the god of Genesis created the moon for this very purpose. These are the views of the priests who penned this creation account.

Thus it is for the Sabbath observance as well. "On the seventh day" means on the seventh day from when the new moon's crescent first appears in the night sky, and by extension each consecutive seventh day thereafter until the next new moon appears, which starts the counting over again. Readers often miss the point of the Priestly writer's seventh-day Sabbath by pointing out that since the moon was not created until the fourth day, God therefore did not rest on the seventh day from the moon's appearance. This reasoning is short-sighted on two accounts. The text of Genesis says nothing about the moon's position or phase when created. But this is itself a moot point, because this line of reasoning misses the mark. The analogy between God resting and keeping the seventh day holy and mankind's covenantal obligation to rest and keep the seventh day holy that the Priestly writer establishes is "on the seventh day." So just as God consecrated and rested *on the seventh day* of creation, so too man observes this holy nature of the seventh day by keeping the Sabbath *on the seventh day* of the new moon's appearance and each consecutive seventh day thereafter. The Israelites were to rest *on the seventh day* as God rested *on the seventh day*. This is our author's message.

At any event, this is yet another example of where and how our so-called modern day Creationists fail to acknowledge, keep, and believe in the Bible's creationism. For according to the priests that portrayed God creating this world and its built-in calendar, not to follow God's calendar as established at creation was blasphemous pure and simple. It was considered a blatant act of blasphemy against God's creation. Apparently however, Creationists really don't care about this either; for they neglect and interpret away this text, *the god of this text*, and his Sabbath every seventh day from the new moon and each consecutive seventh day thereafter! This is not in itself problematic; for we have seen now how this archaic worldview was one that represented the beliefs of ancient Near Eastern priests. It only becomes problematic *and hypocritical* when a group of modern so-called Creationists claim that they believe in this ancient text's creationism when in fact they do not. By contrast, the text of Genesis 1:1—2:3 is an expression of the beliefs and worldview of the ancient priests who wrote it. It does not legitimate the modern beliefs and claims of our so-called Creationists.

YAHWEH'S FIXED FESTIVALS: MORE DISCARDED HOLY DAYS

Although the Sabbath may be the most visible of the creator God's holy days which he established as an inherent part of the created world, according to our priestly author, there are other days alluded to in this creation narrative that were also viewed as inherently sacred. In fact, it is precisely so that mankind (or uniquely Yahweh's people) could know when these holy days occurred in this world that the creator god created, in part, the luminaries, the most important of which was the moon.

> Let there be lights in the domed expanse of the skies to separate between the day and the night, and let them be for signs, and for fixed times, and for days, and for years. (Gen 1:14)

We already saw in chapter 1 that these "fixed times" or "appointed festivals" were part and parcel to the cultic worldview of the priests who wrote this text, and that furthermore they were specifically identified and enumerated in another passage penned by this same guild, Leviticus 23.

> And Yahweh spoke to Moses saying, "Speak to the children of Israel and say to them concerning Yahweh's fixed times/festivals (*mo'adim*) which you shall call holy assemblies: 'These are my fixed times/festivals (*mo'adim*)." (Lev 23:1–2)

Leviticus 23 then proceeds to enumerate Yahweh's sacred festivals, identifying the days on which each holy assembly occurred by the terms already presented to us in Genesis 1:14—namely, by means of the moon.

- The 14th day of the 1st new moon is Yahweh's Passover
- The 15th day of the 1st new moon is Yahweh's Festival of Unleavened Bread
- The 1st day of the 7th new moon is the Horn Blast Holy Day
- The 10th day of the 7th new moon is the Day of Purgation or Atonement
- The 15th day of the 7th new moon is the Festival of Booths

These specific days, like the seventh day from the new moon's appearance, were also deemed inherently holy and conceived of by this Aaronid priestly guild as part of the created ritual order of the world established by the creator deity at creation. Furthermore, each of the above holy festivals is proclaimed as "eternal law." The Israelites were commanded by Yahweh to observe these "fixed times," his holy festivals, eternally. Failure to comply resulted in being "cut off" from Yahweh, his people, and the land. In other words, the moon was created first and foremost according to the priests who penned Genesis 1 so that Yahweh's people would be able to ascertain when these sacred days, these eternal laws, occurred, which were woven directly into the fabric of creation. These eternal laws too, in other words, were deemed inherent parts of the creation, just as our author perceived the sun and seas as inherent parts of God's creation.

At the conclusion of this chapter, it must be stressed that I am not advocating that we follow these texts and their beliefs. That would be impossible. For they represent a worldview that died many thousands of years ago. We live in a world forged of different values, different beliefs, and different perceptions about the world and its nature. My point simply is that modern day Creationists and other Fundamentalists who claim that they believe in the Bible's creationism simply feign belief in these ancient texts in an attempt to legitimate their own subjective claims and beliefs, while blatantly disregarding the claims and beliefs represented in the texts of Genesis 1:1—2:3 and 2:4b—3:24. The beliefs of modern day Creationists, in other words, are just that—unsubstantiated, and erroneous, subjective claims about both the text of Genesis 1:1—2:3 and the world at large. Again, this has been demonstrated by the text of Genesis 1:1—2:3 itself. The text, in other words, adjudicates against the claims and beliefs made about the text and the world by these self-professed modern day Creationists.

Conclusion

The primary aims of this study were firstly to illustrate through a culturally contextualized reading of Genesis 1 and the larger composition that this author originally composed that the beliefs and worldview represented in this corpus of literature were shaped by cultural perceptions and beliefs about the nature of the world held by priests of the ancient world, and secondly to illustrate that the claims made by modern day Creationists about Genesis 1 in support of their own beliefs are neither supported by the text itself nor the beliefs of its author as revealed through the text. Presently, I'd like to touch upon the broader ramifications that these conclusions lead us to consider. But first, let us briefly summarize what this study has revealed about the texts of Genesis 1 and 2.

WHAT THE TEXT OF GENESIS 1–2 REVEALS ABOUT ITS OWN COMPOSITIONAL NATURE AND THE BELIEFS AND VIEWS OF ITS AUTHORS

First, when the text of Genesis 1:1—3:24 is read and understood on its own terms and from within its own cultural and literary contexts, we notice that the text itself reveals that the beginning chapters of the book of Genesis preserve two creation accounts—that it is in fact a composite text. We furthermore saw in chapter 1 that being honest to this text's composite nature and its stylistic, linguistic, thematic, and even theological differences revealed that its two creation accounts were penned by two different authors who held differing views and beliefs about the origin and nature of the world and of man and woman. We additionally saw that each one of these creation accounts expressed beliefs, messages, and worldviews uniquely tailored to the specific culture, geography, social setting, and time period in which these two texts were composed—one written by an educated elite priest of the postexilic period influenced by the literary traditions of Mesopotamia, and the other written by a secular storyteller of the days of yore in the land of Canaan. These stylistic and thematic differences, these competing authorial messages, beliefs, and worldviews were revealed through an objective reading of the texts themselves and from within their own unique cultural perspectives. That is to say the observable textual data and the conclusions drawn from them were reached independently of the reader's religious or nonreligious persuasions. They are drawn from our object of study—these ancient texts themselves in their proper cultural contexts.

Second, we furthermore saw that the texts of Genesis 1:1—2:3 and 2:4b–24 revealed that not only did the authors of these two creation accounts hold differing views and beliefs about the nature of the world and of man and woman, but that these competing views and beliefs were shaped by each author's different cultural and literary contexts. More specifically, it was observed how the description of the creation of the world and of man and woman presented in Genesis 1:1—2:3 was in actuality an explanation of how the world *as its author and culture perceived and experienced it* came to be. That with a proper understanding of ancient literature and the literary conventions employed by ancient scribes, we saw that what the author of Genesis 1:1—2:3 depicts the creator God creating is the world as it was perceived by its author and his priestly guild—not the objective world, but a subjective world, subject to the culturally conditioned views and beliefs of the priestly guild that composed this ancient document. So in the end ancient texts do in fact represent the views and beliefs of ancient peoples and cultures. This really shouldn't have to be argued for.

Third, despite the ardent claims made by modern readers influenced by this text's longstanding interpretive tradition, the text of Genesis 1:1—2:3 itself reveals that it is not the word of God, however one wishes to conceptualize this. I realize the alarming and sensitive nature of these conclusions, which I will address more fully below. But we must, as a culture, start acknowledging these texts on their own terms and that includes not only what they reveal about the beliefs of their authors, but also what they reveal about their own compositional nature and the literary conventions employed by ancient scribes in substantiating their beliefs. So once again what the text itself expresses are beliefs about the origin and nature of the world and of man and woman as they were perceived and experienced by its author and his culture. Indeed, the creation account was written in part *to legitimate* those beliefs and perspectives by presenting them as those of the creator God himself. Yet we saw that one of the literary techniques employed by our ancient scribe was to project or transfer his culturally defined beliefs and perspectives about the nature of the world, his cultural "truths" as it were, onto the deity of his composition so that in the end the god of Genesis 1:1—2:3 creates the world as it was perceived and experienced by its author and his culture. The words of the text, then, were shaped and influenced by cultural perceptions and beliefs held by this author and his priestly guild. They represent *his* beliefs and *his* culturally conditioned "truths" about the nature and origin of the world and of man and woman. This brings me to my next point.

Fourth, the textual evidence of chapters 1 and 2 combined reveals that what the author of this text was doing was crafting an image of God that coincided with and supported his own culturally shaped priestly perceptions and experience of the world. It is no coincidence that in this corpus of literature, and only in this priestly source, Yahweh is presented as advocating through eternal covenants, eternal laws, and other decrees the unique views and beliefs of the Aaronid priestly guild responsible for writing this text. The Yahweh of his composition, in other words, is a literary creation which he shaped in support of his own views and beliefs. Again, I realize the provocative nature of these conclusions, but the fact is that they are drawn from observing the textual data. If we were to compare the portrait of Yahweh and his eternal laws and covenants in the Priestly source with other texts of the Bible, with for example the book of Deuteronomy or Jeremiah, or even the writings of Paul, these conclusions would become even more evident. I'd also like to remind my readers that I am making no claims about God per se. I am not discussing God in any metaphysical, ontological, or theological sense. What we are doing here is simply noting the observable textual data and the literary techniques used by ancient authors and the conclusions this evidence leads us to draw *about the text*. In other words, we are talking about the text and the beliefs represented in that text, and that includes how our author understood and portrayed his god. Thus the text itself and all things in it are an expression of *his* beliefs, *his* worldview, *his* concept of God, and *his* culturally defined perceptions about the world. Our task as mature responsible readers of the twenty-first century is to acknowledge this, and to understand the hows and whys behind all of this. Being honest to the texts is our first and most immediate task, albeit perhaps the most difficult.

Finally, an honest reading of the texts of Genesis 1:1—2:3 and 2:4b–24 also revealed that the beliefs and unique messages of these two authors not only disagreed with one another, but neither do they support the belief claims made by Creationists about these texts *and* about the world! It was textually demonstrated that the claims of modern day Creationists in professing belief in the nature and origin of the world as depicted in Genesis' creation account(s) were in reality feigned beliefs. Genesis 1 does not legitimate the claims made by modern day Creationists, both about the text and about the world. To the contrary, the text itself revealed that Genesis 1 legitimates *its author's* subjective beliefs and worldview—beliefs and a worldview that no longer exist nor are shared by this text's modern readers despite their convictions. Sure, a modern reader may believe in one or two of this text's views, but on a whole we do not perceive, experience, nor live in the world envisioned in Genesis 1. It is a world that properly belongs to the elite ancient priests who penned this creation account.

In other words, the creationism touted by modern day Creationists is not biblical creationism per the text of Genesis 1! Their creationism, rather, is a modern invention, a sham, a gross negligence of the biblical text itself. They have come to value *their own beliefs* about the text and about the world above what this ancient text is claiming about itself, about the world, about the beliefs of its author, and ultimately about God as well.

All of the above conclusions were reached by reading and understanding the text of Genesis 1 on its own terms and as a product of its own historical and literary world—not on the terms nor contexts of later readers. As a result it should start to become clear that what the texts of Genesis 1:1—2:3 and 2:4b–24 reveal about their own compositional nature and the beliefs and messages of their individual authors clash with the claims made about these texts by later readers who forged new interpretive frameworks within which to read these texts. The claims that the texts of Genesis 1 and 2 are making, in other words, are at odds with the ideas and beliefs implied in these texts' centuries-later label "the Holy Book."

WHAT THE TEXTS THEMSELVES CLAIM VERSUS WHAT LATER TRADITION CLAIMS ABOUT THE TEXT

When modern Christians claim that they believe in the Bible what they are actually saying is that they believe in the belief claims made *about* the text by later tradition, and not the unique, once independent, and competing beliefs and messages made by the Bible's sixty some different texts and authors. Sure they might have a specific verse in mind that they do in fact believe in, but in general the assertion "I believe in the Bible" boils down to a belief in the ideas and beliefs inherent in—and created by—this collection of ancient literature's later interpretive framework. And that interpretive framework goes by the name of "the Holy Bible."

Said differently, modern claims about believing in the Bible are often assertions that profess belief in what "the Holy Bible" as a label implies or has come to mean to the reader on a personal or communal level. The believer believes in the ideas and beliefs that have become associated with this centuries-later interpretive framework, and indeed created by it. These include beliefs that this collection of literature is the word of God or written by the holy spirit, that it is inerrant in its entirety, that it is a homogeneous single-voiced narrative or divine revelation—in short, a holy book. Yet these are all later interpretive constructs that reflect the beliefs of readers who lived centuries after these texts were written and often void of any knowledge about the texts themselves, the historical circumstances that produced them, who wrote them, to whom, and why. In most cases, we can even trace when these beliefs emerged and under what external influences. But presently it needs to be recognized that all of these later reader-oriented beliefs come at the expense of the texts themselves and of the once independent voices, messages, and competing beliefs of the authors of these ancient texts.

Let me back up a moment and clarify what I am saying and conversely not saying. First, this is not a book that argues against belief in God. It is not a book that argues against faith in general. In fact, it doesn't even argue against believing that the world was created by God or a god, however one wishes to conceptualize this. Rather, it is a book that argues against holding certain traditional beliefs *about* the texts of the Bible in a day and age when our knowledge about these ancient texts, about ancient literature in general, and about the historical and literary contexts within which these texts were composed reveals that such traditional beliefs are no longer tenable. Why? Because the biblical texts themselves tell us this. Unfortunately, however, the authoritative nature of this centuries-later interpretive framework, "the Holy Bible," and all that this title implies still dictate what this collection of literature is for many readers despite the fact that the texts themselves when read on their terms—not the terms and beliefs imposed by this interpretive framework—reveal that these traditional beliefs are not supported by the texts themselves.

We saw this very fact through our reading of the first two chapters of Genesis on the terms of the text—that is, before the Holy Bible was ever created and Genesis' two creation accounts were codified together and reinterpreted through this later framework. One cannot believe simultaneously in both of the beliefs, messages, and worldviews represented in these two creation accounts precisely because, first, they express competing and at times contradictory messages and beliefs about the nature and origin of the world and of man and woman, and second, they no longer reflect our own beliefs about the nature of the world. When modern readers attempt to "harmonize" these differences away what they are actually guilty of doing is placing their own beliefs *about* the text or those they inherited through that which is implied in this text's later interpretive framework, "the Holy Bible," above the independent messages and beliefs of the authors of these texts. And this places these readers in a precarious situation because they not only place their beliefs about the texts above the individual beliefs and messages of the authors of these texts, but they also display—unintentionally I assume—a certain disdain and negligence for the texts themselves and what *they* reveal about their own compositional nature and the beliefs and messages of their once independent authors. Such reading practices negate our authors' beliefs and unique messages, and replace them with those of the reader!

This particular phenomenon brings me to my last point: this centuries-later interpretive framework, "the Holy Bible," exerts more power and influence upon the reader than the once unique and independent beliefs and messages of this collection of ancient literature's sixty some different texts and authors. The modern tendency to harmonize these two creation accounts together, and by extension toss out the individual beliefs and messages of their authors, exemplifies the power and sway of this later interpretive framework over and above the individual beliefs and messages expressed in the texts themselves. Through the aid of this later interpretive framework, it is the reader who now supplies the meaning and message of the text of Genesis 1–2, and not its independent authors. Indeed this later interpretive framework creates a new author—God himself—for the sole purpose of legitimating the beliefs *about the text* held by its reader which were forged by the interpretive tradition in the first place. Meanwhile the independent and competing messages and beliefs of the authors of Genesis

1 and 2 are relegated to the sidelines, if even that, and the reader now appropriates the text to substantiate his or her views and beliefs *about* the text, and ultimately in this case about the nature of the world as well. All of this happens, of course, without the reader knowing any better, and this is precisely because this is how interpretive traditions work.

The relationship between a later interpretive tradition and the text(s) it purports to re-present is something that I have been interested in ever since I was a graduate student, even prior to my interests in the Bible. What we find in almost every case where a later interpretive tradition is imposed upon an earlier text, is that it is the later interpretive tradition that becomes the authoritative voice in asserting what the "true meaning" of the target text is. The interpretive tradition, in other words, becomes more authoritative than the text itself in determining the target text's meaning. This may not in and of itself be so surprising, but the subversive nature of this interpretive phenomenon is. While innocuously setting itself up to be the voice of the target text(s), the later interpretive tradition actually *steps in for* the message of the text(s) asserting that its message *about the text(s)* is the "true" message of the text(s)! This is exactly what has happened with the relationship between the later interpretive framework "the Holy Bible" and the texts it purports to re-present. In fact, it could be argued that the very purpose and function of this later interpretive framework is to re-present and repackage the message of the text(s) that this later interpretive tradition purports to re-present as the "true" meaning and message of the target text(s). But what is often happening behind the scenes as it were is that this new reading of the target text and the message its interpretive tradition purports it to have are none other than a reflection of the very beliefs and views of this later interpretive tradition's readers, who created the interpretive tradition to begin with! So the "reading" of the target texts through this later interpretive tradition—"the Holy Bible"—only confirms this later readership's beliefs *about the text* as represented by the interpretive tradition itself. Thus, the interpretive tradition moves the meaning of these texts as determined by the texts themselves to the meaning of these texts as defined by the terms and belief claims now imposed by this later tradition. In other words, "the Holy Bible" not only physically transforms this anthology of ancient literature into a holy book, but it imposes ideas and concepts—whole belief systems and a homogeneous narrative message—onto these texts that once expressed unique messages carved from specific historical circumstances that spanned a thousand-year period of vast geopolitical and religious changes. The reader's beliefs are now substantiated not by the texts themselves but by the interpretive framework that now stands in for the texts and their once independent messages. And this is precisely the situation that we find ourselves in with Creationists and the claims they are making about the texts of Genesis 1 and 2.

THE GROWING PROBLEM OF BIBLICAL ILLITERACY IN OUR COUNTRY

The very fact that Creationists can claim that they believe in the creation of the world as depicted in Genesis 1 and use this text to substantiate their own modern agendas and beliefs, when the text itself adjudicates against their claims and makes contrary claims of its own, is just one small example of the growing problem of biblical illiteracy in this country. Part of that problem, as outlined above, is that most readers have mistaken the messages and beliefs of these once independent texts for the message and beliefs that are now supplied and imposed by these texts' later interpretive framework, "the Holy Bible."

But Creationists take their hypocrisy to new levels. Not only do they wish to pawn off their own subjective beliefs about the text of Genesis 1 and about the nature and origin of our world as the beliefs of the author of Genesis 1—and ultimately of God as well—but they also seek to present their unsubstantiated beliefs *as biblical creationism* and advocate that this gets taught in our classrooms! This is not only grossly negligent of the text itself, as has been sufficiently demonstrated, but it also displays *our* negligence as a culture for allowing such practices to even be entertained. For in what other discipline would we allow an individual unschooled in a particular field of study to teach their own subjective beliefs and pawn them off as the viewpoint and beliefs of the primary texts of that discipline? We wouldn't accept this in any other field of study or profession. If we wanted to teach biblical creationism in our schools, which of course as a biblical scholar I have nothing against, then I've just written that book! The educational task was to reproduce an unbiased, objective, and culturally contextualized reading of the worldview and beliefs represented in the texts of Genesis 1 and 2, and to understand them on their terms and from within their own cultural contexts. But to allow individuals outside a particular field of study to teach their own subjective—and religious—beliefs in place of the knowledge that that field of study has accumulated over the past few centuries and to pawn their subjective unschooled beliefs off as the beliefs of that field of study's texts is nothing short of malpractice and should be prosecuted as such. The fact that we as a culture are allowing this speaks to the impoverished nature of education in general in our country and of biblical education in particular.

Another reason for the growing rate of biblical illiteracy in this country is that we have mistaken religious freedom—the freedom to choose, believe, and practice whatever religion we so desire—for the freedom to believe whatever we want about whatever we want. No one would deny the importance of the freedom of religious beliefs. But religious freedom is not the freedom to believe whatever one wants, whether that be about these ancient texts or for that matter about the world. Most beliefs that ancient peoples and cultures held about the nature of the world, including those represented in Genesis 1:1—2:3, have been eradicated or reformulated through an objective study of the world and the knowledge acquired through that study. Likewise, over the past few centuries the objective study of the biblical texts has led us to realize that longstanding traditional claims about these texts are not actually validated by the texts themselves. When our knowledge about any object of study advances, whether that object be agriculture, meteorology, human anatomy, medicine and diseases, Shakespeare's texts, or the texts of the Bible, we cannot just hold on to traditional pre-scientific beliefs when the object of study itself has revealed certain truths about its own nature that clash with longstanding traditional beliefs, no matter how authoritative they've become. Believing that the Bible is the word of God, is an inerrant homogeneous narrative with a single-voiced message, etc. are beliefs that are no longer tenable. Not because I say so. This has nothing to do with subjective claims. Rather it is because our object of study—the biblical texts themselves—have revealed that these beliefs are not supported by the texts themselves! I realize that these conclusions may be discomfiting to many Christians and pose insurmountable difficulties. But we must start acknowledging these texts and their messages on *their* terms, and stop carelessly and hypocritically using them to legitimate our own cultural beliefs, whether about the texts or about the nature of our world. If as a culture our most cherished beliefs about these texts—beliefs handed down and forged by powerful, longstanding and authoritative interpretive traditions—are called into question by what the texts themselves reveal when objectively studied, then we have an obligation to these texts and their authors to acknowledge that, and move forward.

In the introduction to this book, I claimed that the real debate with regards to Creationism was not between science and religion. Rather, it is between what the texts of Genesis 1 and 2 profess on their own terms about the beliefs and worldviews of their authors, and what modern day Creationists pontificate *about* the texts. Despite their fervent claims, the texts themselves have revealed that they do not in fact believe in the beliefs, worldviews, and messages represented in these ancient texts. The biblical text, in other words, adjudicates against the belief claims made by modern day Creationists! Thus it's not science that posses a threat to the ideas and beliefs represented in these ancient texts, but Creationists themselves! They have become the enemies of these texts and of the beliefs and messages of their individual authors.

On a more sympathetic note, I realize that the beliefs of Creationists and for that matter millions of Christians are cherished and extremely significant and important in defining their lives. But we as a culture can no longer tolerate an interpretive methodology that substantiates *our* beliefs at the expense of the beliefs and views of these ancient texts and their authors. That is, we have an obligation to these texts and their authors—not to mention ourselves—to acknowledge their messages, to understand them, and then to confront our misconceptions about them, bravely and honestly. But blindly claiming belief in these ancient texts while being ignorant about their authors' own historical and literary worlds and their competing messages and beliefs is not only negligent, but it does nothing in the way of furthering the human species on both intellectual *and* spiritual grounds. Sincerity and understanding is what is needed, even if that path forces us as a culture to entertain questions and a conversation that most would rather not face.

So in the end the challenge that Creationists, Fundamentalists, and literal Evangelicals face is deciding whether they wish to be honest to these ancient texts and the beliefs and messages of their authors by simply acknowledging them, and acknowledging also that we in this century no longer believe in the same beliefs and worldview, or be honest to centuries-later interpretive claims and beliefs *about these texts* which represent the concerns and beliefs of later readers rather than those of the individual authors of these texts. And if being honest to these texts, their authors, and their beliefs and messages leads us to conclude that our most cherished beliefs about these texts, indeed what have become cultural "truths" for many, are not supported by the texts themselves when read on their terms, then that is the conversation that we as a culture must embark upon, openly, honestly, and courageously.

Bibliography

Avalos, Hector. *The End of Biblical Studies*. Amherst, NY: Prometheus, 2007.

Baden, Joel S. *The Composition of the Pentateuch: Renewing the Documentary Hypothesis*. Anchor Yale Bible Reference Library. New Haven: Yale University Press, 2012.

Blenkinsopp, Joseph. *The Pentateuch: An Introduction to the First Five Books of the Bible*. Anchor Yale Bible Reference Library. New Haven: Yale University Press, 2000.

Campbell, Anthony F., and Mark A. O'Brien. *Sources of the Pentateuch: Texts, Introductions, Annotations*. Minneapolis: Augsburg Fortress, 1993.

Carr, David M. *The Formation of the Hebrew Bible: A New Reconstruction*. New York: Cambridge University Press, 2011.

———. *Reading the Fractures of Genesis: Historical and Literary Approaches*. Louisville: Westminster John Knox, 1996.

Coogan, Michael, ed. and trans. *Stories from Ancient Canaan*. Louisville: Westminster John Knox, 1987.

Cross, Frank Moore. *Canaanite Myth and Hebrew Epic: Essays in the History of the Religion of Israel*. Cambridge: Harvard University Press, 1997.

———. *From Epic to Canon: History and Literature in Ancient Israel*. Baltimore: Johns Hopkins University Press, 1998.

Dalley, Stephanie, trans. *Myths from Mesopotamia: Creation, the Flood, Gilgamesh, and Others*. Oxford World's Classics. Oxford: Oxford Paperbacks, 2009.

De Pury, Albert, and Thomas Römer, eds. *Le Pentateuque en question: Les origines et la composition des cinq premiers livres de la Bible à la lumière des recherches récentes*. Paris: Labor & Fides, 2002.

Dever, William G. *Who Were the Early Israelites and Where Did They Come From?* Grand Rapids: Eerdmans, 2003.

DiMattei, Steven. "Adam, an Image of the Future Economy: Romans 5:14 in the Context of Irenaeus' Christological Exegesis of Genesis 1:26." In *Greek Patristic and Eastern Orthodox Interpretations of Romans*, edited by Daniel Patte and Vasile Mihoc, 135–53. Romans through History & Cultures 9. London: Bloomsbury T. & T. Clark, 2013.

———. "Biblical Narratives." In *As It Is Written: Studying Paul's Use of Scripture*, edited by Stanley E. Porter and Christopher D. Stanley, 59–93. Atlanta: SBL, 2008.

———. "Moses' ΦΥΣΙΟΛΟΓΙΑ and the Meaning and Use of ΦΥΣΙΚΩΣ in Philo of Alexandria's Exegetical Method." In *The Studia Philonica Annual: Studies in Hellenistic Judaism 18*, edited by David T. Runia and Gregory E. Sterling, 3–32. Atlanta: SBL, 2006.

———. "Paul's Allegory of the Two Covenants (Gal. 4:21–31) in Light of First Century Hellenistic Rhetoric and Jewish Hermeneutics." *New Testament Studies* 52.1 (2006) 102–22.

———. "Rereading Aristotle's *De interpretatione* 16a3–8: Verbal Propositions as Symbols of the Process of Reasoning." *Ancient Philosophy* 26 (2006) 1–21.

Doorly, William J. *The Laws of Yahweh: A Handbook of Biblical Law.* Mahwah: Paulist, 2002.

Dozeman, Thomas B., and Konrad Schmid, eds. *A Farewell to the Yahwist? The Composition of the Pentateuch in Recent European Interpretation.* Society of Biblical Literature Symposium 34. Atlanta: SBL, 2006.

Finkelstein, Israel, and Neil Asher Silberman. *The Bible Unearthed: Archaeology's New Vision of Ancient Israel and the Origin of Its Sacred Texts.* New York: Touchstone, 2001.

Friedman, Richard Elliot. *The Bible with Sources Revealed: A New View into the Five Books of Moses.* New York: HarperOne, 2003.

———. *Who Wrote the Bible?* New York: HarperOne, 1997.

Hamilton, Virginia. *In the Beginning: Creation Stories from Around the World.* Orlando: Harcourt, 1991.

Heidel, Alexander. *The Babylonian Genesis: The Story of Creation.* Chicago: University of Chicago Press, 1963.

King, Thomas J. *The Realignment of the Priestly Literature: The Priestly Narrative in Genesis and Its Relation to Priestly Legislation and the Holiness School.* Princeton Theological Monograph Series. Eugene, OR: Wipf & Stock, 2009.

Knohl, Israel. *The Divine Symphony: The Bible's Many Voices.* Philadelphia: Jewish Publication Society, 2003.

Lance, H. Darrell. *The Old Testament and the Archaeologist.* Guides to Biblical Scholarship Old Testament Series. Minneapolis: Fortress, 1981.

Leeming, David Adams. *A Dictionary of Creation Myths.* Oxford: Oxford University Press, 1991.

Lemche, Niels Peter. *The Israelites in History and Tradition.* Louisville: Westminster John Knox, 1998.

———. *Prelude to Israel's Past: Background and Beginnings of Israelite History and Identity.* Peabody: Hendrickson, 1998.

Levine, Baruch A. *Numbers 1–20: A New Translation with Introduction and Commentary.* Anchor Bible. New York: Double Day, 1993.

———. *Numbers 21–36: A New Translation with Introduction and Commentary.* Anchor Yale Bible. New Haven: Yale University Press, 2000.

Levinson, Bernard M. *Deuteronomy and the Hermeneutics of Legal Innovation.* New York: Oxford University Press, 2002.

Matthews, Victor H., and Don C. Benjamin, eds. *Old Testament Parallels: Laws and Stories from the Ancient Near East.* Mahwah, NJ: Paulist, 2006.

McKenzie, Steven L. *How to Read the Bible: History, Prophecy, Literature—Why Modern Readers Need to Know the Difference and What It Means for Faith Today.* New York: Oxford University Press, 2005.

Milgrom, Jacob. *Leviticus 1–16: A New Translation with Introduction and Commentary.* Anchor Bible. New York: Doubleday, 1991.

———. *Leviticus 17–22: A New Translation with Introduction and Commentary.* Anchor Yale Bible. New Haven: Yale University Press, 2000.

————. *Leviticus 23–27: A New Translation with Introduction and Commentary.* Anchor Yale Bible. New York: Doubleday, 2001.

Pritchard, James B., ed. *The Ancient Near East.* Vol. 1, *An Anthology of Texts and Pictures.* Princeton: Princeton University Press, 1973.

Propp, William H. *Exodus 19–40: A New Translation with Introduction and Commentary.* Anchor Bible. New York: Doubleday, 2006.

Schniedewind, William S. *How the Bible Became a Book: The Textualization of Ancient Israel.* Cambridge: Cambridge University Press, 2004.

Seely, Paul H. "The Firmament and the Water Above: Part I: The Meaning of *raqia'* in Gen 1:6–8." *Westminster Theological Journal* 53 (1991) 227–40.

Smith, Mark S. *The Early History of God: Yahweh and the Other Deities in Ancient Israel.* Grand Rapids: Eerdmans, 2002.

————. *The Priestly Vision of Genesis 1.* Minneapolis: Fortress, 2010.

Sproul, Barbara C. *Primal Myths: Creation Myths around the World.* New York: HarperOne, 1979.

Thompson, Thomas L. *The Mythic Past: Biblical Archaeology and the Myth of Israel.* London: Basic, 1999.

Van der Toorn, Karel. *Scribal Culture and the Making of the Hebrew Bible.* Cambridge: Harvard University Press, 2007.

Van Seters, John. *Prologue to History: The Yahwist as Historian in Genesis.* Louisville: Westminster John Knox, 1992.

Watts, James W. *Reading Law: The Rhetorical Shaping of the Pentateuch.* Sheffield, UK: Sheffield Academic, 1999.

Winslow, Karen Strand. "Understanding Earth." September 25, 2009. http://biologos.org/blog/understanding-earth.